To my one and only lo ♡ P9-CFD-716

Merry Christmas, 2006

J-cakes

PUBLISHED BY
PRINCETON ARCHITECTURAL PRESS
37 EAST SEVENTH STREET
NEW YORK, NEW YORK 10003

FOR A FREE CATALOG OF BOOKS, CALL
1.800.722.6657.
VISIT OUR WEB SITE AT WWW.PAPRESS.COM.

EDITING: JENNIFER N. THOMPSON
DESIGN: DEB WOOD

SPECIAL THANKS TO: NETTIE ALJIAN, NICOLA
BEDNAREK, JANET BEHNING, MEGAN
CAREY, PENNY (YUEN PIK) CHU, RUSSELL
FERNANDEZ, JAN HAUX, CLARE JACOBSON,
MARK LAMSTER, NANCY EKLUND LATER,
LINDA LEE, KATHARINE MYERS, JANE
SHEINMAN, SCOTT TENNENT, AND JOSEPH
WESTON OF PRINCETON ARCHITECTURAL
PRESS —KEVIN C. LIPPERT, PUBLISHER

LIBRARY OF CONGRESS CATALOGING-IN-
PUBLICATION DATA

HINES, BABBETTE, 1967–
   LOVE LETTERS, LOST / BABBETTE HINES.
      P. CM.
   ISBN 1-56898-478-2 (HARDCOVER : ALK.
PAPER)
   1. LOVE LETTERS. I. TITLE.

   HQ801.3.H56 2005
   306.7—DC22

2004013471

LOVE LETTERS, LOST

BABBETTE HINES

PRINCETON ARCHITECTURAL PRESS
NEW YORK

FOR CARLOS, MY SWEETHEART

I am interested in stories: the stories we tell about ourselves and the stories people tell about us. Despite our attempts to construct a certain identity, to present a deliberate face to the world that cannot be penetrated or undone, there is often a contradiction between what we would like the world to see and what it insists upon seeing. When I first began collecting love letters, I believed I had found an ideal arena in which to explore this contradiction. Where better, I thought, than in a love letter, would one be likely to present a specific (if not altogether idealized) portrait of oneself? Whereas in real life you may be boorish and stinky, within the safe and comfortable confines of a letter you have the chance to distill the very best of yourself, with none of the more obnoxious or merely annoying traits that would surface should the wooing be successful. Realizing that I would have no opportunity of comparing the person with the persona, I was still certain that I would find, buried in the language of love, evidence of this prevarication. As it turns out, I was almost entirely wrong.

It is easy enough, in a moment of passion or in the face of someone else's desire, to say something that you really don't mean in an attempt to coerce or console. Even in an e-mail, which is easy enough to send (or delete) with a single touch, it is not that hard to invent or declare feelings that may not stand the test of time. Letters, if those found here are any indication, are a different story altogether. Perhaps it is the act of putting pen to paper or the time required to distill thoughts into written words, but what emerges from the process is the truth. It is easier, after all, to deny what you have said than what you have written; even if you are fairly certain of your reception, it takes an act of bravery to reveal what is truly happening in your heart. It seems that if you are going to be that brave, you might as well be honest.

If a picture is worth a thousand words, then what are a thousand words worth? With a few swift strokes of the pen, a portrait is painted of an entire relationship. While words record the present, the past and future are to be found in the spaces in between. In photographs it is easy enough to envision the lives of the couples caught in the act of being couple—the photo is the first line of the story. With a letter we have the second and the third. And yet it's not the entire story, since they are inevitably written in the private language of lovers. There are veiled references to mistakes, and sex, and sorrows. There are secrets forever hidden from our curious eyes, which is fitting in that we are only visitors, having not actually been invited. We know them and yet we don't. At the very least we recognize them or, perhaps, ourselves in them.

The very act of writing a love letter is both selfish and selfless. Selfish, or at least self-interested, in that the writer has an almost desperate need to be known and understood, which has very little to do with the recipient and everything to do with the writer. Yet it is selfless in the way that love must be selfless, in the desire to please and comfort the one you love. There is then an important reciprocity, an underlying implication (I love you because you are lovable), which further compounds and strengthens the relationship beyond the words themselves.

There are as many ways to express one's love as there are ways to feel it. And yet the vast majority of the writers contain themselves to a few simple words and phrases: I love you, I miss you, I am lonely for you, I wish you were here, I wish I was there, I think about you every single second of the day. They are clichés, and then again they are not, for these words spoken in truth continue to wield the same power, no matter how often they are used. Within this common framework and language there are infinite variations, representing the many characteristics of love itself: theatrical, petulant, romantic, or

occasionally even a little dull. The selection here reflects these variations, from those sweetly tedious letters (the contents of which are only of interest to the recipient, containing the intimacies and shared knowledge that often hold a relationship together) to those full of such delight and amusement that they transcend their circumstances. There are those sending out the first tentative root, hoping for fertile soil; those reflecting love rejected or ignored; and those, like Kenton McCoy's, that are so fine that you can not help falling a little bit in love yourself, though they were written almost ninety years ago, and besides, he only had eyes for his own Sweetie Patsy McCoy.

We are constantly and eternally seduced by love, if the preponderance of romantic comedies, romance novels, and popular songs about love and loss are any indication. We watch and read and listen, we fantasize, and then, maybe, sometimes, we compare and wonder if our relationship, our love, is as passionate, as eternal, as heartfelt and tender. These letters are so engaging, so comforting, because they actually are our love; they are real and have not sprung fully formed from someone's imagination. They reflect actual lives and relationships, and from them come the knowledge that in this dangerous and satisfying dance, we are not alone. Every possible feeling, from anxiety to euphoria, has been felt before by countless individuals and will be felt by countless more. These letters, once lost, serve not just as emissaries of love, but of comfort. At least to me.

KENTON McCOY,
FINANCIAL AGENT

THE INDUSTRIAL OIL &
REFINING COMPANY

1002 NEW DANIELS BUILDING
TULSA, OKLA.,

Monday evening.

Jenks Okla., Aug. 18, 19

My Dear Sweetheart:-

That's such a pretty name for you:

I have just finished a full day's work, and now
I will have a nice time all by myself, with you. So far and already,
I have had two most awfully good letters from you and sent you three
or four from this end.: It's lots of fund writing to you, just like
boys and girls-

Your letters are so full of most interesting;
humanly interesting news and so vibrant with optimisim that I most
would forego the pleasure I get out of writing you, in order to have
all the fun coming ffom you to me, if it were not just quite as
true that you get lots of thrills from the ones you get from me.

There now! have I made myself clear, and do you
see between the lines that I love you very dearly and more constant
from day to day. And it grows on me like - whickies! Every day
there's a new crop - of little loves.

The atmosphere around Jenks just at present, very
much resembles the spring crop which sprang up shortly after "Coys"
blew in and oiled the wheels of industry. If you find that I repeat
some of my "achievements" from day to day, it is perhaps because I
am proud of them. Neverloes, seven old dry oil wells lie prostrate
tonight on the river bank, having their vitals carefully withdrawn;
measured, numbered and labeled, with two distinct crews going after
the remaining portions of the leases'anatomy.

I mentioned I might stew up some kind of pot-
pori for weeums, so to-day I laid a little bait, right here in this
very little city, and long comes a feller and says, says he, "that
looks good to me, I811 take you on for that" and if he does, we will
be in the oil business for ourself. I like this action stuff!

Me thinkin, G Patsy, G, I'm a bachlor and you'r
a her bachlor, and we're both cooking our own beans and fixin up our
own business, and meby long'l come somethin and make us both rich
and everything.

Tuesday morning I am going to Tulsa to get the
money for the Carmac lease? they phoned me to-day to bring the papers
and close the deal, so if that goes, it will be score number one.
The first week on the ground.

I am going to turn in now and take this to town
with me early tomorrow and tonight I will hug you very close to me,
and love you ever so much, Sweetie dear.

Fondly and affectionately,

Kenton

I love do love you Dear,

do you remember this?
You don't know?
I do, it's when we went for
a walk in los regatas.
What a beautiful time, right?

ha ha ha ha ha ha ha ha ha ha ha

Your wife who adores you
with all her heart

       tomi

D   Bremerton.Washington
                                     November 16,1943

Dearest Wife, And Daughter..
     Iam sure you will be surprised to receive such letter
     I am proud to have the pleasure toimforme you yOur
husband is Abig shot in theU.S. Navy at this instant
     I know it will be hard for you to beleive but Iam
now A seaman Ist. class Idraw about I6 dallars Per.
Month And our Navy Scrues Us out of the rest but
Theres one consleation We can take it canT We?
     When this war is over they can kiss our a-- cant
they/? No Iwouldnt give them such Atreat to even see
yours Would you?
     I would sure like to bewith you and my kid this
 Christmas maby lcan, lets hope so, lwould like to
 be with you right now, Buts thats impossiable seems
like If l am in the states l have hopes and l will be
 l think
     l am on Astand by watch to night A nd as l had A l
 lot of time l thought l would jump on this typewritt
-er and beat you out Aletter Youknow it is,nt any
 trouble for me to type , as l play the paino so Well
sSweetheart I guessIі*   I had better close
     Ihopee* YOu will enjoy this letter
               Bye now   _** KISSES for YOu And Betsy
          I love You   ************************
               Your Husband ************************
          LTbnard Lynn Miller ***********************
     The Patrotic Sucker   ***********************
                    ****

****

                    The End
                    ILove You
               Good Night BE Sweet

Excuse all mispelled words I'd get a
word Ralf finished + then I'd have to look
for the rest of the Keys, + get the wrong one

March, 28, 1945

Dearest Sam:

Received two of the most beautiful cards and letters from a most beautiful girl, yes sir honey I really needed them both, for today I was in the one of the worst moods since the time I left you in Phili, yes honey I felt like chewing nails and I did chew two if you know what I mean, and I know you do.

Sam darling if there were someway I could have one look at you, I know I would feel so much better, gosh honey I am missing you more than ever our last meeting dosen't seem like it ever happened.

Sam I received the money $200 but if you will send me another 25 of those _____ & _____ I will _____ it back to you, Sam did you know you are not only the best but the only girl in the world? You are to me honey and you know that to dont you?

Without a doubt my love without you I would be no more, without you the world would be glad to get rid of me for I would

March, 28, 1945

Dearest Irm:

Received two of the most beautiful cards and letters from a most beautiful girl, yes sir honey I really needed them both, for today I was in the one of the worst moods since the time I left you in Phili, yes honey I felt like chewing nails and I did chew two if you know what I mean, and I know you do

Irm darling if there were some way I could have one look at you, I know I would feel so much better, gosh honey I am missing you more than ever, our last meeting dosen't seem like it ever happened.

Irm I received the money $200 but if you will send me another 25 of those kisses and hugs I will send it back to you, Irm did you know you are not only the best but the only girl in the world? You are to me honey and you know that don't you?

Without a doubt my love without you I would be no more, without you the world would be glad to get rid of me for I would worry it to death.

Irm do you know I love you so much that it hurts and so much it is wonderful at the same time, are you that bad or is it just me.

Irm I know by now you have received lots of mail from me or you should have and honey I think you will receive it better now. I am proud of you keeping your lenten intentions and I know you kept them for the both of us, for I haven't done anything. Sorry to hear that Johnnys mother is in the hospital, give him my sympathies. Your ring darling and the words inscribed are like a prayer when you wear it, it was for me any way.

Darling tell Don I'm waiting for his letter and tell that wife of mine that I love her to great for comfort, gosh I would love to see you.

Reds is Don. Birthday the 9, 10, or there abouts if so I will send his card as soon as you let me know.

My darling I love you and will forever.

Always,
Marty

Wylie, Texas
Jan'y 9, 1928.

Dear Douglas; Will answer
your letter which I received this
evening. Was surely glad to hear
from you and some of the things
you said made me feel happier
and causes me to have more
confidence in you. You seem to
be absolutely fair in your
dealings with me and that is
the thing that I appreciate so
much.

Really, I wanted you to be
with me Sun! but I wanted
you to keep your promise

Dear Douglas:

Will answer your letter which I received this evening. Was surely glad to hear from you and some of the things you said made me feel happier and cause me to have more confidence in you. You seem to be absolutely fair in your dealings with me and that is the thing I appreciate so much.

Really, I wanted you to be with me Sun. but I wanted you to keep your promise I feel that if you will keep your promise to them you will to me too. I don't feel that I shall mind waiting for you for I feel that you are worth waiting for. The fact that you want to wait until you can take care of me makes me feel that I can truly have faith in you.

Well I feel this way if you find that you don't love me why by all means tell me and I shall release you from any obligations to me. I shouldn't want any man unless he thought I was really and truly the one he wanted. I appreciate your attitude in regard to this: but my dear, if you truly love me and want me and I find I can trust you as I feel now that I can why I shall not want to ask for any release from my promises.

Somehow I won't feel that I am being deprived of any thing by accepting you and forgetting all of these other boys who I might go with. Of course there are kids who are friends but that is all. I told mother one time this fall that I was through with 'em all and didn't want to marry but I believe I feel differently since I've met you. And I feel that I shall be glad to be true to you and look forward to the time when we can have a home of our own. And I too can possibly work toward securing some of the things for it. Say, did you know I too am part Scotch? Ha! Ha! Well, I am any way and appreciate the farsightedness which you seem to exhibit.

And I feel that every thing will turn out alright and that we can and will be happy after awhile. And we can be now if we can feel just secure in each others love. As you said the other night maybe you do have a hard job. Well it may not be so hard after all. The only thing you will have to do is just be true to me and love me. That is all I will ask and that will work the charm. And I don't want to disappoint you either. I am going to try to act in such a way that you can always care for me. I shall be fair with you. And try to be as considerate and reasonable as a human can be.

I don't think that I will be losing any thing by becoming engaged to you but really feel that I shall gain much love, happiness and the dearest man in all the world to me. Say, you may think I am just a kid but I've seen enough of life to be willing now to look on the more serious side of it and accept my share of the responsibility of making a happy home. And even if we have to wait a while may be it is best and we shall only appreciate each other more for having to wait and knowing that we have been true to each other. Sometimes life appears to treat us cruelly but do you know that usually things turn out for the best after all? At least I like to think they do.

My people liked you. Mother hardly saw you but said she liked your appearance. My daddy likes you a lot it seems. He surely said some nice things about you. He told me and also mother that he liked you. Guess you think I've set out to write a book tonight but I'll be done direckly. Guess you were surprised to find that letter hope I didn't say anything I shouldn't. I hate it that I said what I did the other night was afraid that I had maybe hurt your feelings but dearest, I just had to tell you so you could understand me but Harry dear, I shouldn't ever want to hurt you. And I feel like I can have faith in you so don't worry about what I said.

I will have to go over to a neighbors house and practice tonight. I am in the next play which our club is to give. We will give the play the 27TH of this month. I must close for tonight.

Lovingly yours
Venna M Donald

P.S. Write often please

Darling:

Please be a good brave girl Honey. It will be most lonesome for both of us but just keep on remembering that I do love you so much and will be waiting to see you again.

I will absolutely, never will cheat on you, honey as I never want to have to give you up.

Be brave and remember we were meant for each other.

I will be thinking of you every minute.

Goodbye Darling

xxx xxx x x x xxxxxxxxxxx

SAN FRANCISCO, CALIFORNIA

Dearest Dag.

I have been thinking things over very carefully and have arrived at the conclusion that you are entirely right and I am all wet.

Simply because I love you is no reason for me to expect a lease on you or your affections, because to you I am only another. It seems to me that my long suit is to continue as your favorite friend and forget my troubles for the time being.

You said that you do care more for me than any other one, and that the longer you knew a person the better you liked them so I still have hopes. Possibly if keep your friendship long enough you may see things differently.

So lets end all quarrels and be the perfect friends we were at first. I am going to be so darn nice to you that you wont be able to help loving me.

If you care to continue our relationship call me up and I will take you to the dance to-morrow night.

Love,

Sal

Friday P.M.

Dear Friend!
By yours of this
morning I find that
you misinterpreted a
portion of my letter, but those
things quite frequently
occur in correspondence when
they do not in conversation
But that is a small matter.
Do not think that I feel
wronged because I surely
do not & feel quite as much
relieved as you or perhaps
more. If you were near
enough I'd say "I'm mighty

Friday P.M.
(July 6, 1917)

Dear Friend

By yours of this morning I find that you misinterpreted a portion of my letter, but those things quite frequently occur in correspondence when they do not in conversation. But that is a small matter.

Do not think that I feel wronged because I surely do not and feel quite as much relieved as you or perhaps more. If you were near enough I'd say "I m mighty glad you feel as you do <u>cause thems my sentiments</u>" and we'd shake on it. Never allow yourself to think that I ever considered your intentions serious, for had I then I should not have gone with you as I have been doing. This statement will prove itself in time. "Get me?"

I am dreadfully sorry if you have called up any time when you choose not to, you made the dates, not I and you should have known me well enough to know that if you did not care to come then I should not want you to.

As I now think we understand each other perfectly and both feel well pleased, let's drop it and you may feel very sure that my attitude toward you is that of a pleasant and kindly nature.

Sincerely,
Mary

oo.oooo oooooooooo ooo oo oooooo

kisses for you sweetheart,

Springdale, Iowa, Dec 7 '95

My Dear Elija.

I am at home safely,
found them well and mother
came clear out doors and put
her arms around me and said
"My boy! my boy" just as I
told you she would, They
do not look much older than
when I saw them last.
I arrived at Cedar Rapids
this morning at 1:30 and had
to get up at 5 again, found

My Dear Eliza,

I am at home safely, found them well and mother came clear out doors and put her arms around me and said "my boy! my boy!" just as I told you she would. They do not look much older than when I saw them last. I arrived at Cedar Rapids this morning at 1:30 and had to get up at 5 again, found a cousin waiting for me, I got here in time for breakfast. Just father, mother and cousin Minnie I told you was lame.

Al and Mary are coming to dinner and it is now after noon, so I have to hurry with this and tell you that I love you ever so much. I had to shave myself this morning and it hurt worse than your slaps. My pet how strange it seems that we are fifteen hundred miles apart and that we will not sit together this evening.

I told mother this morning that I left the best little girl behind that ever lived and she asked why she didn't come along, so I told her you were teaching school and couldn't. I do hope you can see them, my parents, some time. they would like you I know. Father and I went out to see the town a little while ago, and passed the place where Miss Johnson used to live, a pretty little cottage, and not the slightest feeling of old times came over me, nor the least desire to enact any of those scenes over again.

My heart and thoughts fly away to feast themselves upon a scene enacted by just you and I at 3290 eyeanets st. and it makes me happy to think that they are soon to be enacted over again by the same actors. I cannot express all the love I have for you, life with your dear self by my side will be happy. I have showed them the copper and told them I was to deliver it to a friend in Ohio. They do not know why I am going. With love and fondest wishes for your safety until we meet again.

Your Lover,
Horace

Jany 2th 1863

Mary I am again to
send you a few Cts
in money for postage stamps
&c & if you happen down
to the Penn. Please have
Our Picture taken &
send me send it in a
case for this one is
spoilt it is hard keeping
a Picture in the Army
I spoiled the case &
it is most all spoilt
but the case we can
get where this come from
& just as handsome ones
in my oppinion what
Do you think about it
Mary you Spoke about
Betsy She has played out
she has not written

July 29, 1863

Mary I am agoine to send you a few Cts in money
for postage stamps etc. and if you happen down to
the town please have your picture taken and send
me. Send it in a case for this one is spoilt it is hard
keeping a picture in the army. I spoiled the case
and it is most all spoilt. But there can be more got
where this come from and just as handsome ones in
my opinion. What do you think about it. Mary you
spoke about Betsy. She has played out. She has not
written to me since I told you what I did about it
but I understand She is about to step off with
another felow. I am happy to know you are so keeping yourself for my sake. And I am happy to write
you the Love which I have for you. Pen cannot tell
it to you, but I live in hopes of seeing you again.
I always took a notion to you evory since the First
time I ever seen you. You will still live in remem-
berence of me and I will keep myself for Molly.
Molly is my true Love and no other but her can
I love. Prey tell to me her heart and if she will keep
her reward. Urs Ever True Molly D Babcock. Mary
write what you are a mind to and none but me
will see it.

Urs truly

Oct. 13, 1919
Inglewood

Dear Ethel Talbert
   I have herd that you
were sick. I hope you are
well now. I wish you come
to school soon. I have chang
my seat. I am the last one
in the row now.
      From
  Albert Honeywell

Sunday   Jan. 28,1940.

Darling;
        Shall I begin with Saturday night?
        Just before leaving the studio I booked a $50 wedding. That
means I get $18 next week and a steady job. Old man Brunel Practic-
ally kissed my hand. (You say ass, your not so wrong there). I
worked like a bastard all day. I stayed until 8, I could have left
at five:30 but I knew how I would feel not seeing you.
        When I got home I felt very low. Ab finally came in with th
heavy cake under his arm and I made a sarcastic remark. That finish-
me off with the both of them. I took my shower and just lay in bed.
I was even too miserable to write. Mother who was feeling better
came into the room and sat on the bed. She asked me why I looked as
I did(you know what happens to my face when I feel blue) but she
claimed I looked pretty anyway. (Don't laugh when I get sleep I hold up)
        All that sympathy was just too much for me. I just broke
down(like a V Ford) . She put her arms about me and kissed me. It
is so long since I have had her consolation that I immediately
stopped crying. It was like a novelty and like a child I looked up
at her with new wonder and admiration.
        She told me not to feel bitter about my fathers attitude
because he felt it was for my benefit. She positively holds no
grudge against him for his past mistakes in his treatment of her.
        She is definitely the most loyal person alive.
        We were talking about Grace and Ab and she said Grace must
be a little blindbecause every time a deposit is supposed to be put
on the furniture he becomes ill. With that crack I laughed like hell.
        Although Mother is ill she is sharp and shrewd and from
time to time proves unusually observant.
        When we finally got to the subject of us two she admitted
you were a nice person but that someday all your niceness would
vanish if we ever had to struggle.
        She is so dear sometimes.in her very frank and undressed
statements that it hurts me greatly to think we have so little of
her. Her good moments are so rare,
        I went to bed feeling much better.
        This morning I arose early and want to see Bornstein , the
photographer. I can work three evenings a week and will average
about $18. It is proof passing for home portraits on L.1.
        I walked from 143rd street to the house and really could
have walked another two miles if I hadn't gotten hungry.
        I am debating whether to take a course at night in adver-
tising or work for Bornstein. Darling which will be more beneficial?
I want to get out of the stinken photography business. Allin all
what I do amounts to a row of pins. (Since you came into my life) I
will wlak walk in your shadow,so make it strong.
        Have you seen Jimmy Jemail down there? Anything with him
is just something for the moment , no future.
        Should you come across something small dearest but with
possibilities as to future, scrutinize it carefully and don't be too
independent. Beggars can't be choosers.
        Darling, enough business.
        Tell me dearest, do you miss me as I miss you?
        Thank God tomarrow is Monday. I hope I have very little
time to spare. Since you have gone Brunel has greatly profited . I
sign up ten dollar orders left and right.
        The day passes but the evenings are so damn long.

Oh well, we should console ourselves with the fact that there is
beauty in our feelings. To feel intensely is to really be alive
and that we are.

A Strauss waltz is playing on the radio and I canjust close
my eyes and feel your kisses in my face, your breath is warm and
your handsgentle and I tenderly stroke your face delightful
delightful----.

In true Pearl manner this is the height of'mental masti-
bation'. Do you imagine the same.

I think I'll walk or something, being alone with these
thoughts is too much.

Morning   8:45- -Monday - -subway

Darling,

Received your epistle and it left me breathless. Each
word was a dripping delight of sweet nectar. I've read it three
times already and each time the flavor is better, I just can't
seem to get enough of its fragrance.

If I ever had an idea you wrote delightful letters before,
I was dead wrong. In comparison, -- well there is none-- before
you were playing the cello, but now you are playing a beautiful
orchestration of the flute , harp and violin.

I've gotnto confess.

Emma brought the letter to me while I was eating my cer-
eal. iI read the first paragraph twice and two tears came right
down my face. I had to stop eating. I flew to the bedroom and in
solitude finished reading, least I should bring shame upon
myself because of my emoetions, amidst a lesser understanding and
colder elementof the house.

I never hope to feel anything sweeter(but there is always
something more and new always) than the first taste of your love in
wt written words.

It seems every word you wrote stood out in bold type and
jumped up and kissed me every time I looked at it.

Someday when we have found our peace and security , I want
you to-wtiwrite and write and write///// I want the world to get
the plaesure of your words. Dearest you are a er master craftsman
when it comes to putting human emotions in readable form. And when
you want to you can kill anyone with you bold and-muma human humor.

) Will write more in the studio)

Evening   8 P.M.

Just finished dinner. Wanted to write during the day but was very
very busy. I hoped for it and damn it I got it. The day was bitchy
and disgusting. Every customer handed me an argument until they
practically wore me down to a frazzle(I know it's hard to imagine)

By the time I got home I felt as if i was coming from the
battle field, There was a curse in my heart and a snail on my
mouth and I was ready to fight at the hint of an   angel.

The sooner I get out of this racket the better. I think I'll
start studying advertising next week.

I broke the record and read your letter again, its beauty
lingers on and on.

My fathers bitterness draws me closer to you. You have
taught me love and gaety and I am against anyone who has none of it.

You know dear we place a particular value on things we
have to work so hard for and that value can never be substitued.

Your journey down there means so much, I hope the God's of
fate smile kindly upon us just this once.

Darling we've got to win , I won't lose and so you can't
because we are ONE.

I am always confident and so dear you are too.

A great dealthat I have wti written this time is dull, like
my life without you right now, but letting you in on it inevitably
makes you part of it and that you are.

Every moment away from you seem s like a year and a year
would seem like a century and yet I would wait that year fre for
you, if I had to.

During the time we have been together we have woven an
intricate pattern of beauty and colorand like two zealous artists we
have carefully guarded it and watched it grow. It keeps on growing
and every complicated design makes it more alluring and each new
shade added gives it more-eeler life, until the two artists are so
wrapped up in it that we are forever bound to it/

Im going to sleep now darling — a million
kisses I throw I to you tonight — every night you are
the last one I think about before I close my eyes &
the first one in my mind when I open them —

9: AM — Tues — Subway —

'Mornin Darlin —

Got your letter & as usual
When I receive a communication from you I
feel lighter —

The subway ride always passes so
much quicker when I am writing to you —
I might take some pictures today & if I do
I'll send them out before the end of the week —

Dearest try to rest up a bit. Job —
hunting is nerve wracking so get to bed early —
I have been getting plenty of sleep
but I am not over- joyous & I am so
anxious to hear that you have landed
something — a friend of mine by name of Gertrude
Brooks is a good friend of Ben Gaines
of the Damon- Vandesbiet — shall I have her write a
letter to him? Darling let me know what you are
doing — & write — I'll not take any excuses
about your being busy —

Your,
Ros —

Oct/7 1947

Hello Honey:
I recieved your letter last
night. Sure was glad to hear
from you. but I don't like
the business about Leona
do you know where the guy
can be located, And don't
you think I should come and
take care of that. I am
asking you because, you can
think things like that out.
And I can't about. all I can
do is get action, that is
what I would have done if
she had been here with me.
Probably, some one would have
gotten in to trouble pretty quick.
Honey if you killed me, I say so.
I want to do a few things
for you before I take off again
I don't think it will be long
now before they start calling us
back. And My number was
pretty small. I guess we will be
over.

Helo Honey:

I recieved your letter last night. Sure was glad to hear from you. but I don't like the business about Leana do you know where the guy can be located, and don't you think I should come and take care of that. I am asking you because you can think things like that out. and I can't about all I can do is get action, that is what I would have done if she had been here with me. Probably, some one would have gotten in to trouble pretty quick. Honey if you kneed me, say so. I want to do a few things for you before I take off again. I don't think it will be long now before they start calling us back. And my number was pretty small. I guess we will be called by our old numbers. If they do get us again. Don't you worry though about it. I wont ever change where you are concerned even if I do have to go through another war before I can have you back. I am going to cut my last cutting of hay tomorow it sure is selling good if I was sure I would have enough to run on. I would sell this cutting. My calves are realy doing good I sure wish I had 20 or 25 head. guess I will get them if I dont have to go back in the army though. Honey I cant think of a thing to write. So will close for now.

Answer Real Soon
        I love you
                Myrl

Dear Ruth,

Will you please forgive me for the way I acted last night? I am realy sorry and promise not to do it again. I didn't know I was so mean until I got to thinking. Wont you please forgive me?   David Gottfredson

P.S. I hope you and Eva dont do what you were going to. Sunday.

David

(I.- L.-Y.)

Name C. Beckwith A-38630-13
Box 368, ... Calif. Conservation Center—
So. Branch, Chino, California
Date .... Feb. 23 ...., 19 66

My Darling

Thank you ever so much for the lovely letter of Sun. I

received it tonight & your thoughts are wonderful. In all reality

we should be very thankful that we are able to see & hold one

another every week-end - Do you agree? Honey, we both know that

one day the doors to my freedom will open to me once again, so

therefore, we should be conserntrating on our future & not our past,

we do have wonderful visits with each other & our time should not

be wasted. We all have our hearts set on moving to Mass. & like we

say, "a whole new life for ourselves" - No more prisons or jails for

yours truly. Above all "Mary Honey," I do want to make" you & our

little-ones" happy & also, I want too be a good husband to "you" & a

good "Daddy Chuck" too "our children" - You understand - Right?

When I wrote you & told you Sweets, "that I've never loved anyone as

I do you," I mean't what I said. For your precious love & understanding I am so very greatful, believe me. Do you forgive me Honey? I hunger so much for "you & our little-ones" God only Knows, how much. When it comes to "you & our little-ones" Honey, many times, I do feel so helpless, but then again I say, "God willing, I will make this all up to "my Honey & our children." If they will all still want me when I am released from here & only "you & our little-ones" have my answer to this. Remember "Mary Honey," always, that I love you very much & forever will. We can talk more on our future at our visits-OK? Oh & as for my opinions, we will also discuss when we meet again. Shall I be looking to see my one & only Fri. afternoon? We will have very much to discuss-Please Honey? Please tell "our little-ones" that their "Daddy Chuck" sends along his love & misses us ever. I do pray that you are all well & in the very best of spirits "God Bless you - Does "our Ray, Steve or Pam" have the Flu Honey? Have they closed "our little-ones" schools yet? I pray they are over their sickiness & all feeling well once again. You will Keep me posted to how "our little-ones" are doing-OK? Have you seen "your Mom" lately? Would you please give her my regards? Oh, I'll let you Know when I hear from my Mom or Carol again-Have you Knitted them lately Sweets? Would "you" or "our little-ones" miss being on the Water-Front (Lake Quinsigamond) when we return to Mass.? Honey, our trip back, we can call some-what of a honeymoon-OK? See, lets hope I don't get too many "Head-aches" on our trip back to Mass. (smile) I love you. Are you resting when-ever you can Sweets? Your rest is so important. Well Honey, after this letter, I will shower & shave & get ready for another day - Everyday brings us all that much closer - Right? And our day will come-Now! (smile) Please let me thank you "Mary Honey" for "our precious little-ones" - Remember that you are all on my mind & I love you all very much - Sweet dream's Hon. I'll be looking Fri. to see you - OK? "Goodnight Beloved & "God Watch Over" you & our Babies" Alway's —

All my love Forever —

"Your Chuck" xxxxxxx

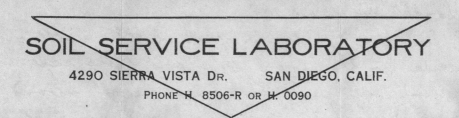

Oh, Sweetheart—

Your two letters have done as much for me as last week-end. Somehow, I think we're as close in our letters as we are together. You see, I know you more through your letters than I do through you. Sometimes your letters give me the "thrill" I spoke of, sometimes they make me happy and gay and sometime they put me in a sort of stupor in which I just sit around and think of you and go over the things we've done together. Oh, darling, I do love you and I want you; some day, dear, I'm going to have you, too. You're going to be mine and mine and mine! Now you underline "Love". Does that mean what I want it to? You said you could say that but not "All my love", but you've added that too.

It's so hard for me to write this to you dear; what I want to say can't be put on paper. I must be holding you in order to convey my thoughts to you.

When you write in your little notebook I'd
be pleased to have you tear out those pages and
send them. One can't be very careless about writing.
I know myself that when I re-read some of my letters
to you I'm not satisfied with the way they sound. If
I had to put them away and then re-write them
I'd leave out or add to, as the case may be, until
they wouldn't have my original thoughts in them.

I can't say the things I want to, dear, so I'd
better close this with so many of your questions
unanswered. About all I can say is I really,
really love you, Berkeley. Please believe me sweetheart,
I love you more than anything in the world. Oh,
my Berkeley, I did kiss your name and I kissed
the lipstick but it's so cold and dry and they
didn't kiss me back.

All my love to you

Bud.

P.S. Please excuse the color combination of
the stationery and envelope. Maybe I'm getting
careless first.

My love —

Bud.

Wednesday morning,
August 27, 1919.

My own Dear Husband:

I'm tickled
pink—so pink that it
affects the paper on which
I write, and I'm sure when
this little missive blows into Jenks town the tickle
will still be in it and the
pink will still survive.

Anyhow, the
cat's out! The beans are
spilled! Every last bean — I'm

My own Dear Husband:

I'm tickled pink—so pink that it affects the paper on which I write, and I'm sure when this little missive blows into Jenks town the tickle will still be in it and the pink will still survive.

Anyhow, the cat's out! The beans are spilled! Every last bean—I'm going to be married. Sh'h'h' it's a secret—this morning I got a letter from my dearest friend, and he told me that the last of this week my Prince Charming was coming to woo me—to love me and kiss me and hug me, and, although he dreams it not—to wed me, for, in the still and solitary hours of the day, and the woozy, wondrous, dreams of night, have I planned and set my trap—dressed it in bewitching robes of rose, perfumed with the musk of music,—and into it will I entice my Lockinvar (with a sugar cookie—'n everything.) But keep it dark, for ah! woe is me— I must no longer a spinster be. D'posh a' voo!

Last night I had company. Grandma Forsythe, Mrs. Forsythe, Winifred, Helen, and Mary Lee and Auntie Forsythe. Auntie Forsythe had two new phonograph records which she asked if she might hear on my Victrola as she has none upstairs. I played my s'pise and Whispering Hope and they all enjoyed it very much—they stayed about an hour and a half.

Pinky and I'se going bye bye now. I'm going as far as the Post Office down town with Pinky, and then Pinky's going to Oklahoma to vamp an oil magnate and entice him to Denver town—coming home with him in his berth—

naughty Pinky; and I'm going to shop for pretties to ensnare him when he arrives—bad me—there's nothing I won't do?

Love
Patsy?

Form 2020—10-12-13—200m.

TELEGRAM

Carthage,Tex,
Feb,18,14.

Dear Miss Jessie;-

      Your card received today, was surprised, but Je
I like surprises, dont you?
Suppose Mc has talked with you since he got my last letter,
and your card was the result, if I had known you were perman-
ately located there, I would have written you, but I tho't maybe you were just there on a visit, now what about it, are you
only visiting, or are you staying there, and what do you do,
if anything?
I'm away out in the jungles here, working for a pipe line CO,
its gets rather monotonous too at times, and a fellow takes
the blues and wants to get out where he can see something again, but thats an impossibility here, but I had better not
write like this, (my first letter too) else you will think I'm
a chronic kicker or an old grouch, and of course I do not want
you yo form that opinion of me.
I suppose Mc has told you of my work also the nature of it, and
where I'm located, so will not give you any information along
that line,Ha ha, it wouldn't be interesting to you anyway, I
dont suppose.

TELEGRAM

Form 2020—10-12-13—200m.

Mc and I are great friends, we worked together for a long while,
and a better fellow I never knew, I feel confident that his cousin is the same to, else he would not speak of you as he did,
I suppose you two have great times there together, going to
shows and such, sure wish I could be there with you and have a
little joy-time for a change.
I took a vacation about Xmas started once to visit Mc, but changed my mind, now I wish that I had done so,
Well as I told you before, news is very scarse here, on account
of being in an out of the way place, so you write, then I'll
have something to write about.
Would be awfully glad to correspond with you, and sure wish
that I was personally acquainted with you, but that cannot be
for a time at lease, so lets consider ourselves as already
being acquainted, what do you say?
  Write soon..

                              Yours,

Dec 5 - 1950
Wonson, Korea

Dearest You;

Just a note to you to say I love you in
case this doesn't turn out for us. We're going to
try a quick hop & hit 'em once more. We'll see
how much good it does later on. We're in pretty
bad shape as of now but between us & those
loveable Jarheads will rescue our worthless
army some how. Ought to leave 'em in & make 'em
fight but they'd probably give up more equipment
than the whole Chinese army has of its own & then
surrender too with out a shot. They should be sent to
Siberia for 4 or 5 years just for drill.

Wish I had more time but we're setting off Wonson
at 12 to nite & every thing has to be out & on board. Then
will let the chinks have it the hard way & I hope they
all freeze. Much 'round the clock turn to and these
sweaters sure are the ticket.

Mary Xmas and Happy Anniversary honey rite now
its the best I can do until later. I've got some thing
to send for you but the mail service has stopped
except for a letter or two until we see wheth'r we'll

wives love. Sure wish I could see you but maybe it's better this way - I can keep my mind on what I'm doing better this way.

      Pray a little honey - I think I will —
          In haste with love
              Jimmy

Dearest You,

　　　　Just a note to you to say I love you in case this doesn't turn out for us. We're going to try a quick hop and hit 'em once more. We'll see how much good it does later on. We're in pretty bad shape as of now but between us and those loveable jar heads we'll rescue our worthless army some how. Ought to leave 'em in and make 'em fight but they'd probably give up more equipment than the whole Chinese army has of its own and then surrender too without a shot. They should be sent to Siberia for 4 or 5 years just for drill.

　　　　Wish I had more time but we're setting off Wonson at 12 tonite and every thing has to be out and on board. Then we'll let the chinks have it the hard way and I hope they all freeze. Much round the clock turn to and these sweaters sure are the ticket.

　　　　Mary Xmas and Happy Anniversary honey rite now it's the best I can do until later. I've got some things to send for you but the mail service has stopped except for a letter or two until we see whether we'll win or lose. Sure wish I could see you but maybe it's better this way—I can keep my mind on what I'm doing better this way.

Pray a little honey—think I will—
　　　　In haste with love
　　　　　　　Jimmy

9/22/82

CFI.152—FLORIDA STATE SERIES

Hi Pretty One;

A stop over here
in Panama City for
a few days to rest
and fish on my way
back from New Mexico.
On my way to West
Palm Beach to get set
for winter months. Love
ya all. Hope to see
you soon. Pop

American Egret, one of the many tropical birds in Florida.

CURTEICHCOLOR® 3-D NATURAL COLOR REPRODUCTION (REG. U. S. A. PAT. OFF.)

PANAMA CITY · FL
PM.
International
23 SEP
1982

United States 13c

Post Card

Miss "Deb"
11 Brook St
Chelmsford, Mass.
01824

Box 277

Dear Daddy,

We love you very much.

We are having fun. Come home soon.

Your 2 sweethearts

Mama and
Christy

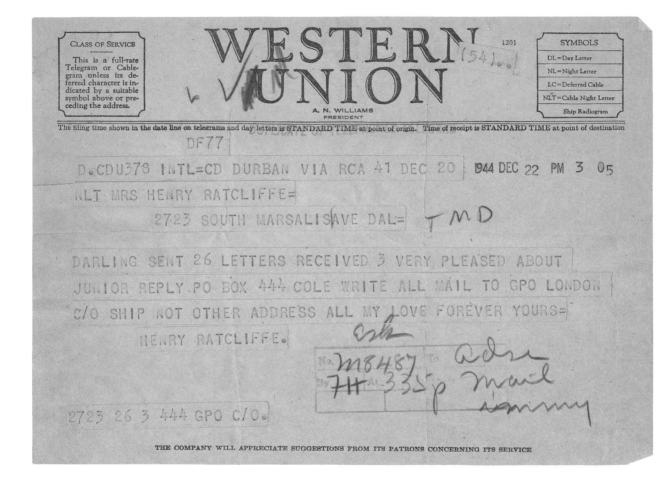

WESTERN UNION

CLASS OF SERVICE

This is a full-rate Telegram or Cable-gram unless its deferred character is indicated by a suitable symbol above or preceding the address.

A. N. WILLIAMS
PRESIDENT

1201

SYMBOLS

DL=Day Letter
NL=Night Letter
LC=Deferred Cable
NLT=Cable Night Letter
Ship Radiogram

The filing time shown in the date line on telegrams and day letters is STANDARD TIME at point of origin. Time of receipt is STANDARD TIME at point of destination

DF77

D.CDU378 INTL=CD DURBAN VIA RCA 41 DEC 20   1944 DEC 22 PM 3 05

NLT MRS HENRY RATCLIFFE=

2723 SOUTH MARSALIS AVE DAL=

DARLING SENT 26 LETTERS RECEIVED 3 VERY PLEASED ABOUT
JUNIOR REPLY PO BOX 444 COLE WRITE ALL MAIL TO GPO LONDON
C/O SHIP NOT OTHER ADDRESS ALL MY LOVE FOREVER YOURS=

HENRY RATCLIFFE.

2723 26 3 444 GPO C/O.

THE COMPANY WILL APPRECIATE SUGGESTIONS FROM ITS PATRONS CONCERNING ITS SERVICE

FORM NO. 6B.

WESTERN UNION
(THE WESTERN UNION TELEGRAPH COMPANY)
(INCORPORATED IN THE STATE OF NEW YORK, U.S.A., WITH LIMITED LIABILITY.)

CABLEGRAM

ANGLO-AMERICAN TELEGRAPH CO., LD.   CANADIAN NATIONAL TELEGRAPHS.

RECEIVED AT 22 GREAT WINCHESTER STREET, LONDON, E.C.2. (TEL. LONDON WALL 1234.)

K3292 DALLASTEX 24   1945 FEB 25 A I 59

NLT HENRY RACTLIFFE PURSER   262D

    CARE CAYZER IRVINE AND COMPANY 2 ST MARY AXE LDN

PLEASE GET WELL DARLING I NEED YOU ABOVE ANY ONE BABY ALL

RIGHT WISH YOU WERE HERE NOR REST DOC SAYS MAY HAVE TWINS

BE PREPARED GET WELL NOR TROUBLE FOREVER MOMEE

                        KIKKI RACTLIFFE

Please send your Reply " Via WESTERN UNION "   You may telephone us for a messenger

Dearest darling:

I wrote a six page letter to you yesterday, but Dad
brought it back, it would cost three dollars to send it, and I'm
broke. so I'm sending it to your home. I was terrible disappointed to hear the news of the delay. I have some snaps in the other
letter. Darling I hate to disappoint you but the snaps weigh heavy
I have sort of felt like nothing on earth since your letter,
I had every thing planned for the wedding, but now I feel like
H----. I only hope now that your plans are changed. I sometime
feel like going off the deep end. But if I went off again I'm
afraid you might come in unexpectedly and then I would feel worse
So I just dont know what to do these long day's. I think I'll take up piloting, at least that would get me out, and I might get
to visit foreign country's, or something. I told you so much in
the other letters that I hate to repeat them again, one thing is
that I could'nt make heads or tails of your last letter. the one
telling me of your 8 weeks leave. I dont think that is right.
you should get a little time here I think, of course that is
just my own opinion. Well we will just have to take what we get
and be glad we got it. Another thing, all the new things I
bought will be old when and if we ever do get married. I'd just
as soon be dead as to live in worry all the time, I suppose I'm
destined to be unhappy the rest of my life. It even seems irrat-
ional to be writing all the time, especially when you say you
never see them, I've just been feeding good American currency
to the fishes I guess, You just take a look at the size of these
stamps on the letter. Imagine what a long letter would cost.
Thats why I have been writing on a typewriter, can get more on

the page. I wish you could get a few of my letters, at least one

at every port. and I write more than one to every port. This is

my seventh across. the original seventh is on its way to

86 Out-----. It was a little to heavy for me this week.

I hope you got my cable, I answered your the same day I got it.

I havent the least idea when you will receive this. But I hope you

do get it for a change, You certainly are a grumbly old man.

You seem to think that I never write to you, and I do. Thats what

makes me impatient,. I sold my automobile, last Monday, this is

Thursday night now, and I dont beleive I ever did really need the

old bus, of course they are nice things to have, but I think it

is very unpatriotic to be wasting gasoline these day's,.and

at any rate there are so many busses and trams you really dont

need a car. and besides I can alway's use Pop's car if you ever

accidentally get down here again. Darn it I wish I could see you

how tall are you now? and how much do you weigh, I'm curious

I want to try to picture you in my mind, Yes I remember the

name of our children(to come) Diane, and Henry III (VIII)

naturally they will be twins, or I will not put up with them.

I think Cassandra Diane Ractliffeis a very pretty name.Dont you?

Oh Bobby whats to become of us, the world is absolutely crazy,

what with maniacs trying to run things, Seems the only decent

things these day's are what you have in your mind. Such as family

sweetheart, and faith in your country. But people dont realize

that faith is not enough, we'll have to work and work hard,

what would our lives be without our own way of living? So I guess

I can patiently wait another four years. However I'm not saying

what I'll look like in four more years. I'm going to start school

in a week or so now, the only reason I waited was that I didnt

want to be occupied while you were here, now it makes no differe-

nce. I still havent given up hope. This is all for now darling

just remember how much I love you and how much you love me and

everything will be ok Love and kisses xxxxxxxxxxxxxxxxxxxx xx xxxx

nd ki ses   kkixxxxxxxxx

SAM
DANA

livine!!"

PLT. SGT. H. S. UNDERHILL
N.C.O. IN CHARGE
MARINE DETACHMENT
SOUTHERN CALIF. TELE. SCHOOL
127 SO. BOYLE AVE.
LOS ANGELES, CALIF.
DECEMBER 5, 1943

DEAR DONA,

I just old fashioned enough to try and tell a girl my intentions before I take her out. Please let me tell you a little bit about myself. I was born in New York thirty eight years ago. The only living realitive I have is a sister back there. I have been married and divorced and want to settle down with a nice girl who would appreciate a home and a good husband. After the war I expect to take a trip back to New York, visit my sister and then come back here and build a home in the vicinity of Hollywood

At the present time I am in command of 38 men who are attending the Advanced Telephone School here. I expect I will be stationed here for the duration of the war. I am on detached duty from the Marine Base San Diego and have been sent up here as Top Sergeant.

The people who were with me last night are Mr. and Mrs. Tiedeman and they live at 4342 Shady Glade, North Hollywood. He is one of the instructors at the Telephone and they are both the swellest friends I have ever known.

They would like to have you come out to their home for dinner Wednesday night so that we could get better aquainted that is if you have no previous engagement.

If you would care to go I would love to pick you up in my car and take you out there.

Dona, I am afraid this is rather a clumsy letter but I would so much like to know you better. If you would care to go I will call you up Tuesday night and you can let me know then.

Your hopeful friend,

Herbie

Black Mt. House
August 26th 1890.

Dear Miss Ada

You will think strange
of me for writing these few lines;
but I get to see you, alone, so
seldom, I cannot resist.

And besides I cannot half
express my love for you in words.

Had I the eloquence of Cicero,
or the pen of Burns, it would
be impossible for me to tell you
half the love I have for you.

I love you better than any
living creature, and no one knows,
save the One above, how happy I
would be, if you could return my
love.

When you seem to treat me
cool, my life is a misery to me, and

Dear Miss Ada

You will think strange of me for writing these few lines, but I get to see you alone so seldom, I cannot resist.

And besides I cannot half express my love for you in words.

Had I the eloquence of Cicero, or the pen of Burns, it would be impossible for me to tell you half the love I have for you.

I love you better than any living creature, and no one knows, save the One above, how happy I would be if you could return my love.

When you seem to treat me cool, my life is a misery to me; and when you are the reverse, my happiness knows no bounds.

Oh please don't turn from me coldly.

Will you not give me some encouragement? Can I not yet have some hopes?

I am yours most devotedly
J. L. Slagle

Tuesday evening.

Dear Sweetheart-o'-mine, I
love to call you that, dear;
it just exactly fits, doesn't it?

I wrote this noon, but right
afterward I thought of several
things I wanted to say.
I don't need the money so
if you haven't already
sent it, don't bother. If you
have — all right. The handcraft fee was only a quarter
and I had plenty — es-
pecially since the leaders
don't have to pay the fee.

When you come down
Friday night — I've been
looking forward to Friday
night since yesterday morning,

anyway - when you come,
will you please me a coat -
my red one I guess. I didn't
think about a coat until
just a little while ago 'cause
I got cold. I'm nice and
warm now - with two
sweaters on.

You know - I'm beginning
to feel a little uneasy
about my visitor. It hasn't
shown up yet at all. I
put on my bathing suit
and walked down to the
beach, but I didn't go in
swimming. I don't think
I will all week.

I can scarcely wait till
the Monday - Tuesday - and
Wednesday of your vacation.

Dear Sweetheart-o'-mine,

I love to call you that, dear, it just exactly fits, doesn't it?

I wrote this noon, but right afterwards I thought of several things I wanted to say. I don't need the money so if you haven't already sent it, don't bother. If you have—all right. The handcraft fee was only a quarter and I had plenty—especially since the leaders don't have to pay the fee.

When you come down Friday night—I've been looking forward to Friday night since yesterday morning, anyway—when you come, will you please me a coat—my red one I guess. I didn't think about a coat until just a little while ago 'cause I got cold. I'm nice and warm now—with two sweaters on.

You know—I'm beginning to feel a little uneasy about my visitor. It hasn't shown up yet at all. I put on my bathing suit and walked down to the beach, but I didn't go in swimming. I don't think I will all week.

I can scarcely wait till the Monday–Tuesday–and Wednesday of your vacation. Just think, dear, I'm to have you for three whole days. Oh boy!—Wait until I get you six months twice a year. Do I envy Red and Alice? Oh no—no more than somebody else. That's all right. Kiddo, it won't be long now. Thanks for the clipping.

For some reason, I didn't get a bit excited about Vee. Haha! Maybe you can thank Nap— I dunno.

It's time for stunts now so I'll leave this letter—but not you, sweetheart. I seem to think of you more around the fire than any time—and that's saying lots, kiddo—for I think of you all the time.

This is the next morning, and I'm supposed to be in Discussion group. I tho't I put this in the mail box so it would be sure to go. I'll write again later.

Oh—my visitor arrived last night without much disturbance.

All my love
Doris

I can hardly wait till noon then I'll get your next letter.

1937

Friday morning at 3:15 AM

1939

During the past nine years I've experienced many
and so varied emotions. I've been bodily kicked out of homes
by sorrowing fathers and mothers who were too choked up by
emotion to be interviewed by me concerning their son or daughters
death. They can be forgiven.

I've been cordially received by industrial
tycoons, moving picture stars and guerillas and gangsters who
arent supposed to know the meaning of the word 'good taste.'

But for sheer ill-bred conduct and rank stupidity you
scaled the heights of a brilliant performance by your exhibition
of Thursday evening.

As a rule newspapermen are a calloused group of individuals who can shake off almost anything that befalls them.
But one thing they find difficult to shake off is insincerity of
emotion. Once that dreaded disease seeps into a persons system
there is very little hope held out for that unfortunate. You
seem to have an over-dose of that sickness, and I think you should
take steps to rid yourself of it.

Since you're such a smug and self-satisfied person,
satisfied with your manipulation of the male specie, I know that
you'll beam with admiration when I tell you what you made me
feel like that night. I felt like a humiliated fool who
had been slapped before an audience and then told to run home.

Being a rather amiable sort of guy who likes to laugh
and make his friends laugh, you probably have reached a conclusion
that all you have to do is snap your fingers, sit back and watch
your "friend" Ralph, type 13486 in your collection, dangle foolish-
ly until you have been sufficiently amused. I'm sorry for you.

I may have experienced many emotions of anger, peevishness and stupidity or frivolity in the past, but never, never in my whole life have I EVER BEEN OVERWHELMED BY SUCH A FEELING OF CLEAR CUT DISGUST AT YOUR BOORISH CONDUCT THAT NIGHT.

You know that I've never foistered my attentions on you. I've never demanded that you endure my presence. If you feel that I can be nothing more to you than just an average, run-of the mine acquaintance, please tell me and I'd have a great deal of more respect for you for being honest with me and yourself.

I've never concealed my affection for you, and as far as I'm concerned you're still NO. 1 with me. All you've got to do is tell me that the feeling is <u>not</u> mutual and I promise that I wont commit suicide.

I didnt go out to Jamaica just to make it conven- ient for you to go home and retire. Not only did you ruin my entire evening but you also played havoc with my frame of mind.

Why in hell dont you grow up and stop playing both ends against the middle?

Now that I've gotten all this venom out of my system I realize that all this drivel I've written is quite futile.

Nevertheless, you must feel mighty proud of your psychology in handling the male specie.

Not only have you made me lose my literary and social self-control for the first time since I've been associating with the opposite sex, but you also have given me a terrific head- ache. Since I feel myself refilling with venom, I'd better sign off. I'll phone you Saturday noon. I hope you take this letter in the proper spirit----you see, I'm much to

3------

fond of you, but I'd rather be fond of you from a distance
than keep on seeing you just because you've got nothing to
do that evening and you're eyes are too tired to read the
comic page for laughs.

Stop acting xxx like xx a much-wronged primadonna and
come down to earth, kid.

CABLE ADDRESS
BANKITALY

13044

Bank of Italy
NATIONAL TRUST & SAVINGS ASSOCIATION
HEAD OFFICE

SAN FRANCISCO, CALIFORNIA

Judging from your conversations and attitude, you seem to be in considerable doubt as to certain conditions. Namely my feelings toward you. I am going to take this opportunity to express my true state of mind to you in a few brief but absolutely frank sentences.

I'll tell the world that I love you, honey. I love you with all the good clean, adoration a human being may ever experience. I worship and adore you, Hag. I think the world of you, absolutely. Without you I don't think I would care to go on. I want you Hag and I want you for my wife.

Please don't ever accuse me again of what you have in the past. <u>If I act that way, it is only because I do love you,</u> first, last and always. I will never leave you Hag. Please believe me and lets not argue on the subject farther.

over

Judging from your conversations and attitude, you seem to be in considerable doubt as to certain conditions. Namely my feelings toward you. I am going to take this opportunity to express my true state of mind to you in a few brief but absolutely frank sentences.

I'll tell the world that I love you, honey. I love you with all the good clean, adoration a human being may ever experience. I worship and adore you, Dag. I think the world of you, absolutely. Without you I don't think I would care to go on. I want you Dag and I want you for my wife.

Please don't ever accuse me again of what you have in the past. <u>If I act that way, it is only because I do love you</u>, first, last and always. I will never leave you Dag. Please believe me and lets not argue on the subject further.

Read the clipping and then think how well this would work out with us. I am sure our folks would agree. What say? Lets do it?

If you get time drop me a line.

Much love,
Just "Pal"

Sunday Morning

Jenks, Oklahoma, Aug.24/19

Dear Sweetie McCoy:-

This is the first day in history, that I have
drawn a blank; both trains in from the north and south and my little
box is empty, but I am going to fill up the avoid by writing you
now for I just know I will get a "Jim Dandy" letter from you on the evening train, because I have learned that I can bank on you, 100% plus.

I'm not a bit lonesome honey, because I did not get
a letter, but I just had to tell you about it like a little kid: I get
so many loving wife letters that I would be greedy if I expected one or
two in every mail, but I love 'em just the same.

I've been planning for you or with you ever since
you told me Mae was coming and I know we are going to enjoy it ever so
much, for it is the very first time we have had "company" and it will
be doubly nice because she was your first lover, playmate and chum
and you have kept here so for many years, which is a high compliment
to both of you and I surely hope she will stay with you for a dandy
visit.

If you have not already done so, you might get the
car washed up real nice at some good garage: I think perhaps the one
at Colfax and Park Avenue would be all right, but the one where we
keep Kem now is no good and I would'nt take it to Central, as they
would be apt to slight it since we left there: Have them use some soap.

And by the way, stop at Bennies on Broadway and
have the tires pumped up, and if you meet Mr. Bennie, tell him I am
away and will settle with him when I get home; I think I owe him about
twenty dollars.

Every night when I go to bed - at nine o'clock-
I shut out all the world but you and your pretty home and think of
every thing you are doing and how you look and what you say to me
and go to sleep with the picture bright and cherry and then wake up
happy and glad another day is here and each rising sun marks one
step toward my home and you.

It's easy to work for pay like that.

Sweetie: you may not believe it, but it is the
Gospel truth; I have not associated with any of the "chickens" since
Ethel left: I look them over carefully every day, admire their pretty
"clothes", only once, just once I touched one of them, and the breast
was sunked and the legs were slim and " I dont see what any body would
see in a skinny one anyway" so I dont either and while we are the best
of friends, we dont "associate at the table", but I do feed and cloth
them and the older ones are quite grateful, they lay around quite tempt-
ingly- five or six a day and they'r fresh too.

But we have plenty of every thing; it blows nicely
most of the time and the roads are quite dry and they mix with the wind
and they both come to see me and we have boiled water too for the wind
and the roads seem to get into the well, besides I have ice!

From Piffel, I turn to Pianos and am wondering if Mr. Wilson has sent a man out to polish your new piano? if not it would be so nice to have it done before Mae comes, dont you think?

Now I am going out in the kitchen and get "us" some lunch: let's see what will we have. We have have two pork chops, cantaloupe, bacon, eggs, apple butter, raspberry jelly, tomato preserves (I made 'em) caned corn, can tomatoes, chipped beef, salmon, bread - no butter - just run out . I made some myself last week, before they took the cow away.

Well I wont starve with that commissary on hand - 12 o'clock.

1 O'clock - all fed and flonrishing: Very warm, big clouds gathering; little breeze; more dry rain.

Did Minerva come? Tell me all about it; did she like your home? Was she surprised, what did you do?   Pause----- Here comes Company.

3 O'clock, Company gone, big talk, no money, anybody's business. most popular man in Jenks- phone rings every few hours- Tulsa talks, sorry I sold the old junk, without giving them a chance; Bull & Bull, Junk buyers.

Junk is more popular than jewels, every body wants junk, at junk prices. Lets go on a junket?

I have a pretty girl sitting here smiling down at me from the desk as I write to you, and she sure is heaps of girl for me and she's never jelous of you and always happy and pretty and I'm worlds fond of her; her present name is Patsy Maurine June Pet Sweetie McCoy!

Some day - soon I'm going to lover her u m m, ever so much in Denver town, in her little pretty parlor, an' her dining room, an' her bed room an' her pure white kitchen, and her snow white nitie, on her soft sweet face, an' everything!   Well sposin?

Honey, there is something wrong with this typewriter, it has a way of spelling differently from other people and makes queer sign at the beginning of words or anyplace: But may be that was popular when it was young.

Now it is almost evening and I am going up to the City to get my letter and send this one to you honeybunch and I wish you were going to be right up there to surprise me and come home with me for supper and perhaps get invited to stay - meby all night - meby? But this is'nt a canvass Dear, for I will come to see you very shortly - O' in about -- meby the first, or sooner ?

I am very fond of you dear and want to be with you all the time but have to get shoes for snookems and Kem and they have em mostly in Oklahoma - just now, but other places later on.

Write me one letter after you get this one. Now the cat's out.

Most affectionately your,

[signature: Husband]

[handwritten: Love me sweetie ?]

Dearest Ninette:

In case you have forgotten my name by this time, it is Stanford. You are not the only one who has already started liking someone, because I like you a lot already. I think you especially look cute in red. Do you have dates very often and would your parents let you go out with boys? I know you think that I am sort of old for you but that doesn't make any difference. I'll just say that you are thirteen and you can say I am fifteen. I will be seeing you often.

yours for as long as you like,
Stanford Clark
Sunset High
6-6237
2207 So. Marsalis

Pearl Harbor
Sept. 7, 1945
Fri. P.M.

Dearest Minnie,

I rec'd your letter of the 4th this morning, not bad luck? I wrote one to mother last night and decided to wait and see if I got one from you today, so now I have one to answer.

I am feeling ok so far, didn't get up till about ten this morning, it was rather late when I went to bed. First I will say they have stoped censoring, so now a guy can write a few little things he didn't want some one else to read when it was intended for just one person.

We like to tell our gal or wife we love them which I do and very much believe it or not, without some one else telling all about it. There has been trouble at times over the censoring of letters, the guys that censor mail get together once in a while and tell about the hot letters some fellows write.

It gets back to some sooner or later and then hell is raised. I went to the hospital yesterday to have them look at the fungus but not bad enough to have to stay.

They gave me stuff they treat the ones in there with and I hope it does some good, I have it under my arm and between my legs, close to something you should

Pearl Harbor
Sept. 7, 1945
Fri. P.M.

Dearest Minnie,

I rec'd your letter of the 4th this morning, not bad huh? I wrote one to mother last night and decided to wait and see if I got one from you today, so now I have one to answer.

I am feeling ok so far, didn't get up till about ten this morning, it was rather late when I went to bed. First I will say they have stoped censoring, so now a guy can write a few little things he didn't want some one else to read when it was intended for just one person.

We like to tell our gal or wife we love them which I do and very much believe it or not, without some one else telling all about it. There has been trouble at times over the censoring of letters, the guys that censor mail get together once in a while and tell about the hot letters some fellows write.

It gets back to some sooner or later and then hell is raised. I went to the hospital yesterday to have them look at the fungus but not bad enough to have to stay.

The gave me stuff they treat the ones in there with and I hope it does some good, I have it under my arms and between my legs, close to something you should always like but most times wanted to put it off till the next night. Please don't get angry at what I said or will try and explain.

Honey, I know at times I pestered you when you didn't feel well or didn't want it and I'm sorry. You were always cold and never did once ask me to do it, I could never figure it out. I tried to make you warm and willing in every way I knew

how outside of getting down and putting my mouth and tongue in Johnnies girl friend, I think you know what I mean. Please don't get mad my sweet, we are going to have to be very close to one another when I get home and love each other lots and freely. I'm willing to help you all I can and try not to have you hate it and you will have to be willing to do it not only at night but at other times too.

Any Doc will tell you it should be done day or night when ever you have the feeling you want it. I could tell you things but it would take too much space. Darling we can't go on using rubbers as we did and taking chances, we have a big enough family now and I know I don't want any more, I don't think you do either.

Something else will have to be used besides rubbers or there is no use trying to make out. I want ours to be a good and perfect love Dearest and I know you do to so we will have to get together on things now. I think you should see a woman doctor, they are called geneologists I think. You can find out for sure, and specialize in making diaphrams. I think you would rather have a woman Doc fooling around you and I know I would. They have to take measurements and fittings and I don't want a man fooling around you, outside of me. There should be a woman Doc in Warren or Youngstown that does that line of work. They are trained in that and are as good and better than men.

Ask mother if you want to Honey, it's nothing to be ashamed of and maybe she can tell you where to go and go with you if you like. Bernie had one made and it cost her between $40 or $50 but they are worth it, she told me all about it and said you should have one. That was when we were first married. I hope you wont be angry with me Dear for writing this letter. I do hope you get one Sweet, it takes time and then you would have it when I did get back.

I love you Lots and wish I were home with you now, time goes slow now and will till my time is up. Wish I could get shore duty in the states by the first of the year, at least I would be on the same country as you are and not quite as far away. So my Daughter likes the merry-go-round but it makes Charles dizzy. Tell him he had better get in shape to knock those bottles down, I believe I can even do it. So Nicky tried to kill himself, those kids are too crazy and always have been. Take a good look at the floor these next few months Darling because you will be seeing a lot of the ceiling when I come home. Have to close now and get over on the other side again. It's only 2 o'clock so not doing bad in answering. What say Baby? All my love to you—
I do love you
darn you.

Yours—

Jack

July 22, 1942

Hello "Rebel" (my "rebel" huh)

Met "Indiana" — your messenger
boy. So you were stingy with Sis' cake!
Shame on you — Goodness —
and guess what — I'm not the only
gal that makes "toll house" cookies
for her marine — "Indiana's" does
too.

Darling — please don't concern
yourself 'bout "our little problem"
to much — There's still a chance
(I hope ——) Even if its slim
it exists. So — here's hoping.

I'm writing this note with
your pen — pleased — I
should think so — After all
darn it I'm getting so I don't
puncuate at all — Oh well —
school's rite round the corner —
and I'll have to buckle down
and study to keep up with you —

David — What were you
worried about at dinner (last nite)
Please tell me — and you
weren't rude — after all —
with Dad and I chatting the
way we were — you couldn't
get a word in edge wise — huh

Darling — please don't
worry — Everything's going to be
all right — I've got my fingers
crossed. ————————

As to the insurance problem
I've got too long a name so —
on all legal papers its been
"shortened" to — (hold your
hat) Violet Kuulei'okalani
Hutchins Conard my name's
also Holly, but since mother's
name's Violet I use it instead
of Holly — complicated?
How can my name be Holly
and again not — Frankly

Hello "Rebel" (my "rebel," huh)

Met "Indiana," your mesenger boy. So you were stingy with Sis cake? Shame on you—Goodness—and guess what? I'm not the only gal that makes "Toll house" cookies for _her_ marine—"Indiana's" does too.

Darling—please don't concern yourself 'bout "our _little_ problem" to much—theres still a chance (I hope—) Even if its slim if it exists. So—heres hoping.

I'm writing this note with your pen—pleased—I should think so—After all—Darn it I'm getting so I don't punctuate at _all_—Oh well—school's rite round the corner—and I'll have to buckle down and study to keep up with you.

David—What were you worried about at dinner? (last night.) Please tell Me—and you weren't rude—after all—with Fred and I chatting the way we were to you couldn't get a word in edge wise—huh

Darling—please don't worry—Everything's going to be all right—I've got my fingers crossed.———

As to the insurance problem I've got too long a name so—on all legal papers its been "shortened" to—(hold your hat) Violet Kuuleilo-kalami Hutchinson 'Cause my name's also Holly, but since mother's name's Violet I use it instead of Holly—Complicated? How can my name be Holly and again not—Forget it for now—Someday perhaps—I'll change it to

Holly Hugh Harris—H.H.H. not that it isn't that nice!

Well———

David I can't remember thanking you for the orchid—not that I have to orally 'cause you understand—There's loads of things you feel that you can't express in words—

Bye—

-                    and

Love

Holly

P.S. Hear you 7:45

My love

and

Kisses

Me

Sunday.

My own Richard! My dearest love!

"I now may no longer say to you,
Do you remember our happy days"? Happy days.
No, rather our joyous hours, when in the
middle of a crowd, we felt so intimately
united; or those their more precious hours
when we were alone, far from the world.

Light of heart, and forgetting sorrow,
we have sometimes even danced together;
and now, overwhelmed with sufferings,
we are separated temporarily and I hope
soon to be re-united; and that as
I have shared your joys, I share your
anguish as well, and if I had to choose
between them, it is the anguish I should
have claimed.

I wonder if I ought to love you so much.
It almost amounts to idolatry, however,
this great love of my life has proved a virtue.
Let us pray and love more and more.
I will write every day if only a line.

Good-Bye, dear heart. May God be in
our hearts, and fashion them, according

to his will. Let us always pray,
always love and always gratefully call
to mind our happiness.
Farewell. May we soon meet again;
If you knew how I love you!

Very Affectionately
Evangeline!

March 23/1930.

PHONE EL. 9225

HOTEL ALPS

NEWLY MODERN FURNISHED ROOMS
621 KING ST.

Wednesday, Aug 30 th

SEATTLE, WASH.

Dear Dodo.

I couldn't bear any longer to tell you how unhappy I have been when you seem to let me understand that you don't love me anymore. Last nite, I could not sleep when I saw that your face look very sad. I asked you what was the matter

You didn't want me to know. Perhaps you didn't think I am a very lonely man. I wish in all the world I've got everything to make you happy. Too I don't want you to work in a place like this where men are good & bad.

I am so very much afraid now, that you seem to misunderstand everything about me. I am good & bad

Seattle's Newest and Most Complete Popular Priced Hotel

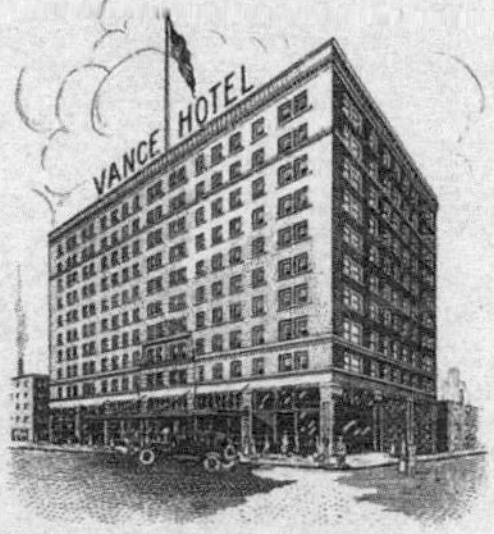

SEVENTH
AT
STEWART ST.

VANCE HOTEL
TIMES SQUARE

Ten stories
180 Rooms
all outside

STEVE T. DALTON
MANAGER

SEATTLE April 2, 1933.

Dearest Dodo;

Just a few lines to let you know how I am getting along in Seattle. I fought a draw last night, but should have had the decision. I may fight another one up here, so in the meantime I'll get in touch with you to let you know how things are.

Honey, I miss you so. Wish you are with me all the time to cheer me up in my melancholy moments. Times are sure dreary without you darling. The days seems years and Oh! how I long to hold you again

"See America First"

Dear Dodo,

I couldn't bear any longer to tell you how unhappy I have been when you seem to let me understand that you don't love me anymore. Last nite, I could not sleep when I saw that your face look very sad. I asked you what was the matter.

You didn't want me to know. Perhaps you didn't think I am a very handy man. I wish in all the world I've got everything to make you happy. For I don't want you to work in a place like this where men are good and bad.

I am so very much afraid now, that you seem to misunderstand everything about me. I am good and bad at the same time. I am very bad when someone put trouble on me or to my friends. I always pick one put on me or to my friends. Big or small. I always love fights and die for it.

Last night when I began to think how disappointed I was to know what your trouble was if there was any. I felt so low for myself. Perhaps you thought you can't use me.

How cruel you are to think of me like this. I wish did been murdered before I meet you.

The every blot of ink in this paper are the blood from my heart. When it seem to break to pieces on account of you that you tell me you love no one but me. I thought you mean it because you told me you love me. I took you very seriously.

I am not so dumb and so intelligent either to understand about women. Who would not be so sweet to a girl like you so beautiful.

Only brave men give their lives for the women they love, but tough coward guys live unhurt, for they love their lives. Last nite I thought there was a guy so particular to you to help you win your respectable. I hope you not to be a nitwit.

Dodo, you use to like me before. We had a lot of fun. Why can't we have this again.

I love you so much for this. Please say those words you used to tell me.

I remain

Yours truly

Ralph

April 2, 1933

Dearest Dodo;

Just a few lines to let you know how I am
getting along in Seattle. I fought a draw last night,
but should have had the decision. I may fight
another one up here, so in the meantime I'll get in
touch with you to let you know how things are.

Honey, I miss you so. Wish you are
with me all the time to cheer me up in my melancholy moments. Times are sure dreary without
you darling. The days seems years and oh! how
I long to hold you again in my arms. Sometimes
I come to think you really don't care for me at all.
But anyway it is up to you if you don't want to
listen to me. What I am telling you are all true, so
please have a little faith in me. Trust me once
more and I'll prove to you that all I say are true.

Garcia and Johnny arrived on the afternoon of the fight, so they were in time to help me
in my corner. Garcia is fighting next week and
I may fight on the same card. So can't tell until
I hear from my manager. Whatever it is, I'll drop
you a line right away and when I get back home,
I'll come over to see you in San Pedro.

Has your mamma started for the north
yet. Give my regards to all, will you, honey. Kiss
the baby for me too.

This is all for tonight as I am a little
tired and sleepy. Will write a long one next time.
With all my regards and love for you, I am

Always your honeybunch,
Star Frisco.

on way to Amarillo, Tex.

4:30 Saturday morning

Beverly Hotel
1330 S. Olive St.
Louse Angeles, Cal.

Darling little bitch;

Your letter reacted upon me like a hamburger to a
starving man. I got a glowing sensation in my chest and it kept on
glowing until it reached my ears and lit them up like Christmas tree.

Please, Dear, dont let strange young men hold your
hand, there's no telling what they'll do with it under the influence
of a tropic moon.

Ultimatum: If Miss Grace Holland has ideas in that
pretty, tousled scalp of hers that she's going to marry Sam Pokrass, tell
her that I'll come East and personally de-sex her with my own hands.
No future sister-in-law of mine is going to marry the craziest son-of-a-
bitch in creation and in that way make him related to me. No siree!

Nevertheless, I like this Ukrainian, piano-pounding
impresario because he is the most alive and genuine person I ever met.
This mad, musical Russian can love violently, hate bitterly, laugh
uproariously, cry pitifully, and all at a moments notice by turning on
or off his temperamental faucets.

Sam is a study in paradoxes. One moment he is suspicious, the next naive. One moment he'll think you're trying to steal
his money and then he'll turn around and throw it away recklessly on
his friends comfort. This Pokrass, though pretty badly neurotic, is
very much the composing genius of Twentieth-Century Fox. His compositions
definitely smack of creative magic. And all this has taken a heavy
physical toll, because Pokrass, living in a continuous state of musical
hysteria, cannot control his facial mannerisms, due to this self-same
neurotic condition. While talking to you his face will twitch in the
most outlandish fashion and cause the listener much embarrassment.

Because of this and other unmarital vices he is
decidedly not cut out (circumsized) for marriage.

This city of Los Angeles is the clearing house of
the poverty stricken, the maimed, the helpless, the consumptive, the
neurotic. It is not a pleasant picture to walk the streets of Los
Angeles and confront living and breathing examples of mental and physical
torture; people who are limbless, others with pain-wracked faces trying
to conceal the agonies racing through their disorganized systems. However,
ix here is Utopia for these unfortunates, because they are able to grab
a little remaining happiness for themselves by basking in this famed
California sun. (The sun hasnt been out for five days, and the natives
are tearing their hair)

These people congregate in the downtown park in
areas they themselves have mapped out and swap yarns about the cheerful things in life. That, my Dear, is the most gripping spectacle of
a "Cheer up, things could be worse" psychology I have ever witnessed.

For that reason alone I think we should be very
contented, and be thankful for our health. I must sound
morbid as all hell, so please excuse as it must be the mother in me and
the lateness of the hour, 5:10 in the morning.

For the first time since I'm travelling for the
Hearst papers I'm very lonely and wish I were back in New York (or Miami).
I havent looked at a woman since I got here. Absolutely not! I creep
into bed with them and immediately close my eyes.

If you think you had troubles in a beauty shop, listen to this
and have a handkerchief handy;

RANDOM THOUGHTS WHILE GOING THROUGH THE ORDEAL OF A HAIRCUT:

Well, its about time I took a haircut, the people at the
hotel and the restaurant are beginning to gossip that maybe I'm a fairy
here's a pretty nice shop, I think I'll go and get clipped...this
son-of-a-bitch who'se clipping my hair doesnt look too substantial...I
afraid a little extra energy expended in the wrong direction will result
in his utter collapse...Jesus! his hand shakes like Jello...of all the
barber shops here in Hollywood, I've got to pick one that's run by a foul
smelling old goat who probably shaved the confederate army...everything
happens to me and just because I loath taking haircuts...Oh, Oh! I'm dying,
he's practically taking off all my hair...but do I do anything about it?...
No!....I want to see how much he'll take off before he gets wise to himself...every clip of his shears clips two years off my age....well, its
almost over now...he's using the razor on my neck, holy mackerel!...Oh God!
I have needed Your spiritual guidance often in the past, but here
is one vital instance where I'd like You to take care of the old guy behind
me...please give him razor guidance and see that he doesnt veer from the
straight and narrow path of my neck with that "colored man's spokesman"
which is clutched rather shakily in his gnarled right fist...well, the
operation is over, and I totter out of the chair, weak, but happy that I
still can get out of there without any assistance....Now all I've got to
do is find a deserted hamlet somewhere in Beverly Hills where I can hide
and keep out of the public gaze until my hirsute adornment is what it was
before I entered this tonsorial butcher shop...If you think child birth
is a torturous process (or dontyou) try watching me take a haircut and
you'll realize that bearing children is like a hop, skip and a jump.

#########

Dear: Tell your Mother that if she doesnt behave herself I'll come down there and give her a spanking in front of all the
Angler's inhabitants.. As far as my friends are concerned, the season is
all over for them and they are back in New York. One worked for the
Associated Press and the other for the Chicago Tribune in Miami.
Dont worry about lining up work for the winter season
in Miami, little Pearl will take care of you when the proper time comes.

I miss you dreadfully. I'm pretty fed up with this
town and may find myself back in New York by May 1st, unless, of course,
I can land a Moving Picture job. And that will be a miracle in itself
because the Industry is a closed shop to those unrelated to the Executives.

Write me a long letter, Dear, and tell me a lot of
intimate things, write quickly because I'm lonely as hell out here.
The bastards out here have me working nights so that I most of the
day, sleeping.   Holy Jesus! Its getting light, and the boys up here
are starting a poker game. I'm leaving for my hotel and some sleep.
Please, God, wont You have Jean Arthur sleeping in my bed when I get to
my hotel?

Regards to your Ma. I trust this letter will give
you a little laugh here and there.

It's 5:55 AM -

DEC · 55

Friday morning
Hollywood, 4/25/41

Coolio, Sr.;

Have just received your Wednesday
letter with photographic monstrosities enclosed.
Those long pants you wear posing with Sylvia
are suspiciously inflated at the bottoms and,
judging from the expression of relief on that pan
of yours, I'd say you just dropped a load
to the ground. You dirty little skunk, you
look positively peaked. I'll bet you don't
even weigh 112 pounds. Where's that
little bachala?

As for the other picture — the
one you posed alone in a seersucker suit —
you look like someone is tickling your
ass with a branch, from the bushes
behind you! Coolie, SKONK, I am
sure that I could positively croak after
seeing my little boolie with her
darling little puss acting like the
devil to show a care-free, gay attitude.
You're so darling, angel. You

Coolio, Sr;

Have just received your Wednesday letter with photographic monstrosities enclosed. Those long pants you wear posing with Sylvia are suspiciously inflated at the bottoms and, judging from the expression of relief on that face of yours, I'd say you just dropped a load to the ground.

You dirty little skunk, you look positively peaked. I'll but you dont even weigh 112 pounds. Where's that little bachala?

As for the other pictures—the one you posed alone in a swim suit—you look like someone is tickling your ass with a branch, from the bushes behind you! Coolie, Skunk, I am sure that I could positively croak after seeing my little boolie with her darling little puss acting like the devil to show a care-free, gay attitude. You're so darling, Angel. You look like a L. J. Katchkala.

In the picture of you <u>alone</u> I expect any minute that you'll pick up your sun suit and show me what's behind the scenes. Remember? You're holding each side of the sun suit and that expression makes me think of those Burlesque strip queens who come out just like <u>you did</u> and start to take off.

Those pictures are making me sizzle. I'm going into the bedroom of my deaf landlady and throw a lay with her. Possibly, I can get away without her knowing about it, you see she's very hard of hearing and her sight isn't too good.

Those darling little legs are so appetizing that I could eat them—if your knees were only clean! And incidentally, what are doing on your knees since I'm gone???

That coquettish grin is driving me nuts (picture of you alone) and I'm sure if I'd been there at the time there would have been much activity between your boudoir and the bathroom.

Please, boolie, don't send me any more propaganda like that or I swear I'll chuck everything and rush home to you.

By the way, how is your finger?? Judging by the paleness of your complexion in the picture you took with Sylvia, I'd say your little finger is working overrtime—on the verityper machine.

One thing is certain—those pictures will never leave my body, day or night. I want you with me 24 hours a day, especially when I feel like laughing. Boolie, boolie, I'd like to smack that puss of yours!!!

Sylvia certainly is getting there, isn't she? I think I'll send her picture to Bernie in the Bronx and have him take care of her.

Seriously, I think I can detect a heavy expresion around your eyes. If that machine is going to affect your eyesight and nerves, the hell with it!! Do you hear me? The hell with it. I'll not have you injuring those darling little "aigalich" (eyes). My Jewish isn't so hot since I got out here.

God, if only you're reading my mind as I devour your likeness from the top of your head to the tip of my shoes. I imagine glorious bits of ecstatic rapture for each part of your body. Your eyes, <u>mouth</u>, ears, neck, chest, breast, arms, pit of your arms, <u>bachala</u>, thigh, <u>backside</u>, <u>pot of gold</u> which is at middles, legs, sides of your legs which are warm smooth and heavenly to the touch of my lips.

All I can imagine is your stark nakedness staring at me, and that glorious little dark fringe of hair at your middle tantalizing my senses until they reel.

Ahem! Certainly is tough about Greece and etc.

For the life of me I can't take my eyes off those pictures. After every third of fourth line I write I have to look at them and discover something new.

I hope this uncensored dispatch doesn't fall into "enemy" hands. I suggest you put it into an envelope, then seal it and put some phoney name on the envelope so as to prevent others from opening it.

I saw Bing Crosby last night and the guy's nearly bald, but still damned good looking.

The weather? Still Typical!

Please don't send me any money from what you earn, honey. You're earning just enough to keep you going.

Honey, it's going to take quite some time for me to finish my book.

You can't merely sit down and rattle off page after page. There's so much planning and plotting to do. Let me do it my way, baby. And the hell with Sloan. If the book is good when it's finished, they'll all be glad to take it. I don't feel too strong to sit down and back away. So <u>please</u> be tolerant and patient and let me bide my time on the book.

My whole heart aches for you, baby, because I love you and miss you horribly.

Ralph

1:30 Just got a <u>special delivery air mail money order</u> from my ma for $10.

Jesus Christ! That last letter I wrote to them must have depressed them badly. you know how low I can act when I want to. Please call my ma as soon as you get this and <u>reassure</u> her that I'm ok. And it wasn't necessary to rush the money to me like that. I still had enough for a week. However, try to be more confident and happy when you speak with her.

What a family I have! Gosh!!

If only your parents were like that to you in other respects. But let's not get into politics again.

You must get highly confused after wading through one of my letters. There is so much explosive matter in it, too, my emotion goes from one extreme to another without the slightest warning. Happy, sad, disgruntled, cheerful, encouraged, downcast, sexy, fatalistic, sadistic.

There was nothing in the envelope except the money order. No letter or explanation. Explain to my ma that she shouldn't get too worried by the tone of my letters. Tell her I still love her and will get her a mink coat with my first 2 weeks salary and that she is my NO. 1 Sweetie— You come second (not really)

Sammy

February 13th 1852

My Dear and most affectionate i will not say lover
but Friend for its my notion you dont care any thing
about me but i still hope you do but to drop this subject
I take the opportunity of leting you know that i am
in good health hoping that this may find you enjoying
the same blessing yourself. It is not very customary for
young ladys to wright the first letter yet you know
it is leapyear now and you must not think hard of it
for it can not be helpt this time for i know you
would never think woth while to send one this course
if i lived the other a rection i would be agrate lickelyer
to get one but so it is and it can not be bettredd now
I herd that you was affended that night you was
here but i did not believeit for i thought of that it
was all a hoax i thought it was only a motting of some
one that is mibling handy and is a little jelous of you
been here but any way i couldent helpt i was sorry
that mother said any thing that night but it nothing
at old womens fables and it is not worth while
mind them for they must be allways talking
but somthing she has forgot that she was young once
herself but we will have toexcue her this time.
My felings was very much hurt and i suppose yours
was the same but i thought you had and i know you
have to better sence than to mind it for i have a hard

My Dear and most affectionate I will
not say lover but Friend for its my notion you
dont care any thing about me but I still hope you
do but to drop this subject I take the opportunity
of letting you know that I am in good health hoping that this may find you enjoying the same
blessing yourself. It is not very customary for
young ladys to wright the first letter yet you know
it is leapyear now and you must not think hard of
it for it can not be helpt this time For I know you
would never think worth while to send me this
course if I lived the other direction I would be a
great deal likelyer to get one but so it is and it can
not be bettered now. I herd that you was offended
that night you was here but I did not believed it
for I thought that it was all a (...) I thought it
was only a nothing of some one that is medling
homely and is a little jelous of you been here but
any way I couldent help it I was sorry that mother
said any thing that might but of nothing but old
womens fables and it is not worth while to mind
them for they must be allways talking about something she has forgot that she was young once herself but we will have to excuse her this time. My
feelings was verry much hurt and I suppose yours
was the same but I thought you had and I know
you have to better sence than to mind it for I have
a hard life of it myself any way but I never think
worth while to mind either him or her for they
have got so used to scolding me that they cant
keep from it when there is any person in and it is
not you more than any body else for they think a

very gradeelle of you or atleast they say so anyway
I couldent think how any person about knew you
were here unless you told them your self and
I know or atleast think that you have more sense
than to do that for I am shure that I never told
any person that you was here and I think that
there was none about the house told any one bad
anall as they are but I dident think anything ofit
for you know the people must be alloways talking
bout something and they may aswell talk about us
as any body else. I couldent think what made you
offended at me unless it was that night I dident
ask you to come back again but I dident know
whether I would be here any longer ornot for
I had some nottions of leaving and another thing
I thought you was offended and would not come
if I would ask you for I never thought you cared
anything about me because I am nothing but a
poor girl and you are not yet you are most welcome to come any time attall to come in the
evening and to stay to ten or eleven oclock they
would say nothing about but to sit up any later
they wont alow me to do with any one I hope that
you will not be offended at me for sending you
this letter for I merely thought that if they would
hinder me from setting with you that they
couldent hinder me from wrighting to you for the
paper and ink is cheap and the time is not so very
presious and the office is not to far off Now I
umbly entreat you not to be offended about this if
you dont think worth while to ancer it or any
thing of it do not let any of the rest of the boys

see or expose me or if you dont think worth while
to read it just throw it in the stove and nothing
more about it What put me in the nottion of
wrighting I thought that small notes was
fashonable and that I might just as well send you
one as any body else you nedent get frightened at
this bad wrighting but my pen is not worth
throwing away and I had no time to get one to
night so you will have to excuse my bad wrighting for I am in a great hury for its nearly bedtime
and I must (…) for to night When Friends and
lovers forsake me I hope the Lord will take me up
My pen is bad my ink is pale
But my love to you shall never fail
But one thing I forgot to tell you that (…) is
preaching again sabaeoth a week and I hope you
will make your appearence and let the folks see
what a young and nice looking gentleman you are
(…) No more at present but remains your

       Friend affectionate
         Friend

alexs-

it is ten forteen sunday
night. i just got home.
i lit three candles and
some insense. stareing into
your eyes in my my car
w/ tool playing was one of
the most peaceful moments
i have shared w/ you.
all of my insanity was
quieted. i felt a very real,
deep connection w/ you.

earlier today you said
"sometimes i feel you are
too close to me". i know i
am, and i love it. i am so
not affraid of this any more.
i heard you on the phone w/
jacob and i was sincerely
happy for you. i am getting to
know you more all the time
and i am constantly overjoyed
you are becomeing you and
i feel like i am a part of it.
when you called me, "pussy"
last night i fell even more
in love w/ you. i can not
really explain that. it was not
as if i enjoyed being called a
pussy, but i really was acting
and you did not let me get
away w/ it. for that i thank
you.
i hope that it was our

Alex—

It is ten forteen sunday night. I just got home. I lit three candles and some insense. Staring into your eyes in my my car w/ tool playing was one of the most peaceful moments I have shared w/ you. All of my insanity was quieted. I felt a very real deep connection w/ you.

Earlier today you said "sometimes I feel you are too close to me." I know I am, and I love it. I am so not afraid of this anymore. I heard you on the phone w/ Jacob and I was sincerely happy for you. I am getting to know you more all the time and I am constantly overjoyed.

You are becomeing you and I feel like I am a part of it when you called me, "pussy" last night, I felt even more in love w/ you. I can not really explain that. it was not as if I enjoyed being called a pussy, but I really was acting and you did not let me get away w/ it. For that I thank you.

I hope that it was our physical contact that was causing you to shake. I love the way you guide my touch. I want to make love to you. I want to feel you rushing through hearts. Yeah, I know that does not make a bit of sence. I have an image in my head of a boulder in a creek w/ clear water rushing over it. I want to be the rock. I want you to be the water. I want you to surround me. I want to fill you.

Alex, you mean the world and the stars to me.

I love you, my heart
GL

P.S. You should compliment me
on this writing it is better than
usual Ha! Ha!

Sizton
Jan 29

Dear Gertrude

Cheerio! &
repeat!! Well, here it
is six o'clock and so
far I have been able to
keep (Cool) calm & collected all day. This has
sure been a wow of a
day, the kind we wish
for sometimes in July or
August. It is sort of
hard on little piggies.
I hope you surely
didn't attempt to walk
home from the bank did you?

Dear Gertrude

Cheerio! and repeat!! Well here it is six o'clock and so far I have been able to keep (cool) calm and collected all day. This has sure been a wow of a day, the kind we wish for sometimes in July or August. It is sort of hard on little piggics. I hope you surely didn't attempt to walk home from the bank did you?

I surely kept cool what little time I was out today. It's a great deal of trouble keeping stock bedded and watered in this sort of weather. Do they keep that bank good and warm on days like this? This fire certainly feels good to me. Every thing is so warm and cozy. Dad and Mom have just left for Jamestown. Nothing would give me greater pleasure right now than have you drop in for a little visit. It's so comfy and restful and your coming would make it perfect.

Mom discovered a broken slat on the wicker couch last evening after we had gone. Ha! Ha! She asked me about it and I sure had a hel-luv-a time trying to explain it. I trotted out my best talent in pervarication and then found myself groping frantically for bigger and better explanations. I finally wound up by telling her I had remembered of something cracking when I sat down on it once extra hard. Can ya beat it. Ha! Ha! Mom's ability to discover things like that and know how they happened is almost uncanny. Thanks for letting me drive my car up to the side of the house last nite. It makes me feel like a priveleged character. If it hadn't been for that I don't believe I would ever have gotten it started. Can

you imagine what happened going home? The car had frozen up again and the temperature had gone way up by the time I had got thru Lizton. I rode and pushed by relays the rest of the way home. When it got hot I shut it off and pushed it till I got warm and then I rode while it got warm and I cooled off. Ha! Ha! I got home about 1 o'clock. When I got home I changed into my overalls and went out to the garage, thawed the radiator out and drained it. I feel sure I never damaged the car any by doing it the way I did but I am wondering why it froze up after having an extra half gal. of alcohol put in it.

Thanks a lot for the banana pudding it was awfully good! no foolin'.

Mom made me fix her wicker couch today. It didn't take very long and that is the piti-ful part of it considering the weather.

I will try and remember to bring over the necessary materials and fix your daven when I see you Wed. If it is possible for me to fix up your burcau I will with a great deal of pleasure, but be sure Bruce isn't watching for I have never had any manual training as I went to grade school in the country and I suspicious that he prob'ly knows a great deal more about it that I.

I have a plan about our Church difficulty. It's only 7:45 but I must retire and try to catch up if I'm to be out Wed. nite.

Yours,

Walter Hines

At Home Sept 9th /85

Charley my Darling Boy"

I would
dearly love to write you a long
letter this morning, but I have
not got time. After I get in school
and get settled I will write you
long letter every week, I was
very much disappointed because
you could not spend Wednesday
eve with one, In your letter
you said you did not think
you could get to spend another
evening with me before I go
away, Now Charley my Boy would
you be so cruel as to let your
little Cos" go away without bidding
her goodby, I would never forgive

Charly my Darling Boy,

       I would dearly love to write you a long letter this morning, but I have not got time. After I get in school and get settled I will write you long letters every week, I was very much disappointed because you could not spend Wednesday eve with me. In your letter you said you did not think you could get to spend another evening with me before I go away. Now Charly my Boy would you be so cruel as to let your little Coz go away without bidding her goodby. I would never forgive you if you would. You must spend friday evening with me won't you? I want to see you awful bad (have a thing as long as from here to (...) to tell you) Send me a good long letter by return mail. You have more time to write than I have. Goodby my Darling. Kiss this right here _____ I kissed it and it will be as good as a kiss in reality. I will look so anxiously for my Boy Friday evening do not disappoint me, and I will expect a good long letter,

       Ever your Coz,
        Maggie

I want most. Get some girl friend to
take them for you. Where ever you have
them taken be sure there is plenty of light.
If you can't or don't want a girl to take
them may be some studio will do it for you
but I don't think so. Don't take the film
to be developed but send it too me and
I'll have it done. There are several
ways I can have it done without embarrassment to you. Now if you don't
want to do this for me say so. It really
doesn't matter except that I'd like to
have them. Finish the roll out on any
poses you want to send. I'll keep the
negatives & prints to myself and show
them to no body that I promise. If it
can be done with no embarassment
to you I can't see why you could deny
me of it. Any man carries pictures of
things he likes & cherishes. I love you
and like those things mentioned the most

…I want most. Get some girlfriend to take them for you. Where ever you have them taken be sure there is plenty of light. If you can't or don't wan't a girl to take them maybe some studio will do it for you but I don't think so. Don't take the film to be developed but send it too me and I'll have it done. There are several ways I can have it done without embarrassment to you. Now if you don't want to do this for me say so. It really doesn't matter except that I'd like to have them. Finish the roll out on any poses you want to send. I'll keep the negatives and prints to myself and show them to no body that I promise. If it can be done with no embarrassment to you I can't see why you could deny me of it. Any man carries pictures of things he likes and cherishes. I love you and like those things mentioned the most so I can't see anything wrong in having pictures of it. Besides their for my use only so please arrange to get the pictures taken by a studio or some girlfriend whom you can trust. The reason I kept putting off asking you was because I couldn't figure out a way to have them finished without causing you embarrass-ment. But sending the exposed film to me and having them finished will not bother you. You will do it for me won't you sweetheart?

Now that's of my mind! I've been on detail the last two night and again to night. Work nights as the days are too hot. Handling what comes from where Art works.

Things are getting better over here but its still SNAFU. Get it?

Well sweetheart I could kiss you extra sweet right now. I'm terribly hard up for you. Oh well we'll catch up when I get home so Goodnight Sweetheart with kisses hugs and my love. I remain

Your affectionate husband
Johnnie

1937

July

Mr. Paul. J. Staunton.
℅ Buffalo Bills Wild West
Bluffton, Ind.

Lockport NY
June 30th 96

My Dear Paul

Your very enjoyable letter
reached me this AM and
I am delighted to hear from
you. really Paul I was afraid
you would for-get to send
me a route card and
what would I do if you
had?

My dear I did not say that
you did not sine your name
to any of your letters I
meant the last letter that
was all. you have always
signed your letter with your
first name. and that is
sufficient.

Oh how lonesome I am just
now when I read the letter
where you say "I wish you
were here". and how I

PS I could not send 40 dollars so
I made it 8 Pounds
Even

Ashland House

H. H. Brockway,
Proprietor.

4TH AVENUE & 24TH STREET

New York, April 7 1903

My darling Wife,

I received your letter dated
Mullingar March 27 My girl
you would not have to
aske me for the money
to come home on. if I
could have got it. I would
have sent it long before
this. The first thing I
done on my arrivel in
New York was to call on
Tom Gill in Brooklyn
and aske him for 50
dollars but he did not
have it. I then wrote to
Campbell and asked
him for 50. He did not
as much as answer
my letter I then wrote
Lund and He did not

My Dear Paul

Your very enjoyable letter reached me this AM and I am delighted to hear from you. Really Paul I was afraid you would for-get to send me a route card and what would I do if you had?

My dear I did not say that you did not sign your name name to <u>any</u> of your letters I meant the last letter that was all. You have always signed your letters with your first name. And that is sufficient.

Oh how lonesome I am just now when I read the letter where you say "I wish you were here." And how I wish I were there I would be so happy. But as you say We cant have every thing that we want in this world and I believe you in this as in every thing else.

Paul isn't it too bad about the Dr. and his wife. She will lose her confidence in him now and I think it is worse to have people mistrust you or not to place confidence in you than to have them hate you. I would ever so much rather they would hate me than to think that they could not trust me, for that would break my heart. Particularly if the one who would not trust me was one whom I loved. What do you think? I hope it will come right when he gets back and I am sure that it will if she really loves him and it is likely that she does or she would not marry him.

It is perfectly lovely here today and I am alone in the depot and how I only wish you were here to share the solitude. Oh Paul, you cannot imagine how lonely I am. You tell me that you see me in the last thing at night and the first thing in the morning well Paul your name is written on my looking glass with a piece of soap and the date when I first met you and your route cards are there also so you see I think of you very often and besides your picture and dear letters but though I did not have those I would still remember. I believe you know that dont you? Please say.

I had an offer of a very good position in Buffalo at $11 per week but my mother did not wish me to accept it so I have not yet. Mamma hates Buffalo, tells me that I would come in con-tact with so many people that she would not care to have me meet. And besides be away from home. It is not in the Western Union. It is in a brokers office on Exchange St.

Tell me what you think about it.

Well my own dear Paul I will close with love. I hope to hear from you soon. I am as ever yours

May

PS I could not send 40 dollars so i made it 8 pounds even

April 7, 1903

My Darling Wife,

I received your letter dated Mulligan March 27. My girl you would not have to ask me for the money to come home on. If I could have got it I would have sent it long before this. The first thing I done on my arrival in New York was to call on Tom Gill in Brooklyn and ask him for 50 dollars but he did not have it. I then wrote to Cambell and asked him for 50. He did not as much as answer my letter. I then wrote Cloud and he did not have it. So you can just imagine how I felt about the matter. I thought if I went to the management of the Show I would not get it as I am a new man and they not sure about my work so when I received your letter yesterday I just made up my mind to go to the front and ask them to advance me some money. I told Mr. Arlington how I was fixed and I would like him to give me 40 dollars. He just took me in the office and wrote me a check for that amount. So far I have found Arlington O.K. This letter will sail tomorrow April 8 and it will reach you about April 16TH don't make arrangements to sail next Saturday April 11TH as I am going to send you about 15 or 20 dollars in my next letter that will reach you about April 20TH. Then you can sail on Wensday April 22 or Saturday April 25TH. That will bring you to NY City the week I am in Brooklyn and in case you should be a day or so late in reaching N.Y. I wont go to Phila that Saturday night May 2. We open in Brooklyn this week of April 27 and Phila week of may 4TH. I think if you arrange it

so as you sail Saturday April 25th it will be O.K. as you wont have to hurry and above all things be very careful of the baby on the tram and on that little boat at Queenstown that takes you out to the ship. Keep them in the cabin of the little boat on the way out to the ship as it is very cold. Enclosed find money order for forty dollars. With all my love your loving husband

Paul

P.S. Look for 15 or 20 dollars more in a day or two

Dear Heart.   April 4/1915

As our train speeds
on toward tomorrow and the
snow capped crest of the Majestic
Rockies raise their highest
peaks to waive a fond farwell
and speak a swift and safe return,
I find myself all but lost in
delicious reverie; snugly wrapped
in a warm blanket of deep
content; willingly resigned
to have lifes harp attuned
anew.

Think not, loved one, you
robbed another to give to me
this cup of joy. I hold no ill
can come to them who scatter
light, and life and love, where
aught had grown before.

April 4 / 1915

Dear Heart.

As our train speeds on toward tomorrow
and the snow capped crest of the Majestic Rockies
raise their highest peaks to waive a fond farewell
and speak a swift and safe return, I find myself all
but lost in delicious reverie, smugly wrapped in a
warm blanket of deep content; willingly resigned
to lifes harp attuned anew.

Think not, loved one, you robbed
another to give to me this cup of joy. I hold no ill
can come to them who scatter light and life and
love, where ought had grown before.

Tis not within the Court of man to say
where Love shall perch and rear her brood!
Perchance, the fledglings in their early flight
should fall and bruise their wings—tis a lesson
wisely learned, and gives them strength and
courage to withstand another flight.

Be well assured that seeds of truth grow
not flowers of grief. A barren soil it were indeed
that should not respond to Love's own kindly
touch which I have found in thee.

Yours to love forever.
Kenton

Monday June 14

My dear Joan

I've thought of you a great deal since my last visit and between other visits. I am deeply attracted to you and would transform this attraction into deep and abiding love. It has been no small thing for me to screw up the courage to ask you to marry me. Its obvious that I'm not in a league with either Mr C or Mr H but I believe I could make you happy and become a loyal and passionate companion. besides it is a different time. This may come as a wild ass surprise but; distance and circumstance remain a barrier to our getting intimately acquainted. I believe that for 51 I'm young in spirit and physical capability and very much want to belong to you and vice versa will you consider and then say yes to my offer of marriage

Love and kisses
Joe

Muskegon Mich
Oct 19 - 1915

My Dearest Dear, -

Recived your
most welcome letter and
i was very anxious to
read it but you fail to
answer the question i
ast you now Dear i
think it is almost
time we had
an under standing as
to what we are going
to do. If you have
the love for me that
you ought to why

My Dearest Dear—

      Recived your most welcome letter and I was very anxious to read it but you fail to answer the questions I ast you now Dear I think it is almost time we had an under standing as to what we are going to do. If you have the love for me that you owght to why you would not hestate one minet. I have offered you as much as any man could now be sure and give me your ancer on this subject in your next letter and dont forget it Dear it means so much to us both. What is the use of waiting a year or more be for we join are hands for life. Well Pleasant you said the weather has been fine here until sunday it rain all day. I work all night satday night I came home and went to bed and got up at noon and then I went to the show after dinner. It was sure fine I wish you was here to go with me. The boys is all here yet that come with me and ther is several other boys from Petoskey two more boys come yestday we are all in the same boarding place. I am going to go on Pine St. wenday night I dont like it here. Well Dear I think this is all for this time I have had a bad cold all week I will close this letter with love and kisses hope to here from you soon from your friend

        William March
          Pine Hurst Hotel
          Muskegon, Mich

Will Ella send me my trunk now or when she come back I am not in hurry for it if she dont send it now you can send it when you go to Petoskey. How did you like my pitcher that I sent you.

TOMMI

The ninety day trial period is almost over. The eve of the honeymoon era. Does that make you nervous.

NOTICE!!

I JUST TOLD YOU THAT I LOVE YOU. I DO, I DO. My stomach is full of butterflies & my ~~stomach~~ blood is rushing hard. I feel like Jesus, I love you see, I did it again. I've been feeling this need to tell you about these gigantic feelings of *LOVE* in my heart but I've been scared. Love is huge and it can grow (just add more love). I've been in love only once before and although I do not regret it, any of it, it did not work out. I wanted to tell you when I came home & saw you & *your* pretty face but I couldn't wait. Last night solidified everything (long story...)

what can I do?
  All I want is to be next to you
I'd take the next bus to your
door but I probably got in
trouble with my boss.

all right, I'll say it
again, then go

I love you
robert
griffith
faraday

Mr Charlie Hay,
Danville,
Kentucky.

Saturday Night,

Charlie I'd

just give most
anything I possess
to have that letter
back I mailed you
last night. I wanted
it back as soon as
it had gone and
specially since I
received your letter—

Charlie,

I'd just give most anything I possess to have that letter back I mailed you last night. I wanted it back as soon as it had gone and specially since I received your letter. I can't say that I meant it and I'm sorry and I'll never say anything like it again—I've forgiven you for last Saturday night a million times and know you'll never do it again and I do believe in you Charlie and can't help it and don't want too —I know the life you are leading is hard and you are so much braver and stronger than I am that I am real ashamed of myself for saying any of the things I did—Charlie you said you had given up all pleasures for me and dearest you know I don't want you to do that for I want your life to be easy and you to be satisfied and happy and everything else in this world and all I ever asked you to give up was things that you couldn't do and be true to yourself. I told you it would be hard and that I was awfully hard to please and maby it would be best and easier for you to forget and if you feel that way for my sake tell me dearest. I love you sweetheart but sometimes feel that I am not worth all the trouble and hardships you are having now and to think that I missed writing to you when my time is my own and that is the least thing I can do to help. Well Charlie anyway I love you and we will never have anything like this to come up again if it just depends on my writing.

I started to go to Brownsville today for the weekend with some married friends but just decided not too, don't know what's the matter with me but guess its just simply that I'm in love with you. Have been busy having a costume made for a masked dance all day, haven't been to a big one around here in so long that I'm real enthused over it and would be so happy if you were only here to go with me.

Must go and mail this before my date comes and Charlie don't forget for one minute that I love you and that I'm thinking of you each day and night and please don't be lonesome 'cause my thoughts are right there with you. Don't worry about not making money this year for I'm sure loving each other as we do everything will come out all right.

With all my heart and love I am,
        You very own
        Anna Moss

June 11th
6 Pm.

My very dearest,

Right now I feel so
completely beaten and helpless
that I should probably
not write. This was such
such a damn unlucky
deal. It makes me mad
the more I think but
yet know everything is
beyond our control. Im
going to kill someone
for this so help me.

I assume you will go
on to Seattle so I will
write you there. Do be
careful dear so that
when the day arrives when
I am able to come back
to you you will be there

for if I were to lose you I should have nothing to look forward to. Tell me all the delightful little details about the growth of positive for is so much a part of us that I want to live through it with you. If God allows us to be apart through his birth kinda pick him up and kiss him for me — but since hospitals are so crowded these days I suggest you make arrangements if possible many months in advance and don't spare the doctors bills for your pre-natal care. Get your teeth fixed! Thats an order. Keep occupied, contrary to anyone's opinion if you are physically able. It's the only way to stay sane.

My very dearest,

Right now I feel so completely beaten
and helpless that I should probably not write. This
was am such a damn unlucky deal. It makes me
mad the more I think but yet know everything is
beyond our control. I'm going to kill someone for
this—so help me.

I assume you will go on to Seattle so
I will write you there. Do be careful dear so that
when the day arrives when I am able to come back
to you you will be there for if I were to lose you
I should have nothing to look forward to. Tell me
all the delightful little details about the growth of
positive for is so much a part of us that I want to
live through it with you. If God allows us to be
apart through his birth kinda pick him up and kiss
him for me—huh. Since hospitals are so crowded
these days I suggest you make arrangements if
possible many months in advance and don't spare
the doctors bills for your pre-natal care. Get your
teeth fixed! Thats an order. Keep occupied, contrary to anyone's opinion if you are physically able.
It's the only way to stay sane.

Don't sit around and be a quiet little
wife either for I want you to be social enough to
keep your self from being an introvert.

You know my darling that I love you
before and beyond all else, except perhaps our
country upon which depends every thing after all.
And that I shall pray for your safekeeping until
my return —and I shall soon.

Love and kisses to Chief and Positive
Your Stinky Husband

Warren, O. June 29, 1900.

My darling Husband.

One letter came day before
yesterday and one yesterday and found
us well but tired. Hope this left you
well. I wish I was there I would rub
that herb on you. You have had it a
long time. We buried Aunt Ann Wednesday. Baby commenced to sing at the
funeral as soon as she heard the organ.
Pa had to take her out. She just rolled
the music off her tongue.

We have finished the scrubbing
part of the house-cleaning. Have to tack
the carpet down in the front room up
stairs, the hall and stair-way. It takes
a long time to finish. I have sewing
to do yet. Aunt Ann's death has put us
back a great deal.

G. L. Bratton, President.
H. J. Withey, Manager.
H. G. Pearson, Secretary and Treasurer.

Offices: 2104 Front Street.
P. O. Box 473.

The Oro Mining Company

CAPITAL STOCK, $1,000,000

Baker City, Oregon, Nov 11 1900

My Darling Wife and Baby,-

Your letter with
Mr Adams draft came last evening, something unusual for your letters to come on
the evening train. About a month ago
some very interesting mining items were
published, if I can get the papers will
send them. We are not getting enough
for stock to afford much expense of
that kind, & suppose that investors
would rather have their money spent
for the good of the mine than to have
it put into high flown newspaper
articles, but as good things are published
will try to send you papers.

Yesterday I sent Mrs. Jenkins 50 prospectuses and a letter as to the Oro stock
hope she will sell lots of it. I have
no specimens to send now. My toe is
well. You make me want to see
Edith very much when you tell about
her. When husband and wife truly love

My darling Husband,

One letter came day before yesterday and one yesterday and found us well but tired. Hope this left you well. I wish I was there I would rub that herb on you. You have had it a long time. We buried Aunt Ann Wednesday. Baby commenced to sing at the funeral as soon as she heard the organ. Pa had to take her out. She just rolled the music off her tongue.

We have finished the scrubbing part of the house-cleaning. Have to tack the carpet down in the front room up stairs, the hall and stair-way. It takes a long time to finish. I have sewing to do yet. Aunt Ann's death has put us back a great deal.

It is very nice to trade with Bentley's for the plums. What are you going to do about canning our cherries? Can you get some one to do it for us? Wish I was there to do it. It doesn't look as though we will be there in time for canning plums.

I am glad you are working this week and hope it will keep up. Hope you will get more soon.

It is very warm here at present. Not too warm at night. It rained yesterday and was very nice after it.

I read mother's letter with pleasure. Glad things are as they are and glad Mary F. is getting along so nicely.

Indeed it would take us long to hug and kiss when we get together again. We are so long away from one another. A year next Thursday.

Yes I wish we could have enough money pretty soon to buy a house etc. and pay for all the time we are separated. I shall be glad to see your flesh filled up with nice fat. My but I would like to be with you and get loved some more. We will all have a good time together. You, baby and I. She is a little fairy, flitting to and fro. I bought her a pair of red shoes and stockings the other day. She is proud of them.

No it won't seem quite like courting days to be together again because you won't need to leave us in the evening. I won't say me as there is a baby in it now.

Well, I am past 30 now. Why, I thought that money would do you good, that is why I sent it. Wish it could have been a larger sum. You can't always depend on friends my dear.

I hope the mining company will be a success as I think a few hundred dollars in a dab will be fine.

Well, I will wait a while longer before looking for something to do to help keep us. Taking care of our daughter and loving you will be plenty to do.

I gave Emma that stock and letter yesterday. She cannot thank you enough. She intends to write and thank you. She was surprised. I think she will try and sell some stock for you. She is so glad. Will she get a dividend on it if the mine proves a success. I love you my darling.

Pa, Ma and baby send love
Lovingly
Your Wife

My Darling Wife and Baby:

Your letter with Mr. Adams draft came last evening, some thing unusual for your letters to come on the evening train. About a month ago some very interesting mining items were published, if I can get the papers will send them. We are not getting enough fat stock to afford much expense of that kind. We supposed that investors would rather have their money spent for the good of the mine than to have it put into high flown newspaper articles, but as good things are published will try to send some papers.

Yesterday I sent Mrs. Jenkins 50 prospectuses and a letter as to the Oro stock, hope she will sell lots of it. Have no specimens to send now. My toe is well. You make me want to see Edith very much when you tell about her. When husband and wife truly love neither cares to change to singleness again even tho misfortunes is theirs. I do not care to give you up even if we are "fa far away" We have tasted of the sweets of married life which we long to again enjoy. I dearly love you, and want to press you to my heart again. The gold surely will not work out of those specimens for it is natural, just as nature fastened it in.

I told Mrs. Jenkins to receive money as promised and I would send her stock with the express understanding that she deliver no stock without receiving the money. Most places would send stock to some bank to be delivered when money was paid, but being pa's sister I thought she could be trusted.

New City Council comes in next month. I do not want City Engineer. I would make more enemies than the work would be worth. I have learned to keep good hours since leaving Butte, do not want to ever get back to Butte ways in that respect. I am nearly always in bed by nine and feel much better for it. We have learned to our sorrow the value of health. You are my own true love, you must help me take care of myself so we can raise our girl aright. Love to pa and ma, and a heart full to my darlings.

Lovingly,
Husband

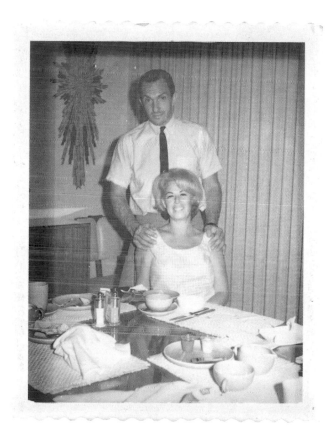

Coopers N. Carolina
Feb. 24th 1891.

My own darling Ada

As the happy hours we
have just spent together are
once more ended; And we are
separated again, I now resort
to my only Means of pleasure,
which is to write to you. Oh!
that those happy days could have
gone on forever; how happy we
would be — But nothing in this
world can last; let it be either
joy or grief. But there is a
great consolation in that pretty
song you have just learned.
"What we have loved, we love forever". My darling I hope you
are quite well by now. I have
thought of you every Minute
since I left, And I can't
tell you how Much I would

My Own Darling Ada

As the happy hours we have just spent together are once more indeed; and we are separated again, I now resort to my only means of pleasure, which is to write to you. Oh! that those happy days could have gone on forever; how happy we would be—But nothing in this world can last; let it be either joy or grief. But there is a great consolation in that pretty song you have just learned: "What we have loved, we love forever." My darling I hope you are quite well by now. I have thought of you every minute since I left, and I can't tell you how much I would like to have stayed another day. But I was almost obliged to go, else I would have stayed.

But I guess you got on with the game of cards about as well without me, as you would have with me.

I have all the pictures fixed very nicely, in frames; and am awful proud of them. Mother likes them very much. She sends her love to you and said to tell you she can send your rose down the next time I come. And she has an apple geranium for you too. Tell Lula Mother said she thought her awful pretty—And I don't think I ever saw her taken on so over any picture, as she did over Dora's—She thinks it awful cute.

I made a frame for Dora's picture this morning; and I think it real pretty—It is made of a very dark red plush, and trimmed with light red ribbon. I am going to make two more, as I have enough of stuff.

Ada my darling I won't write much tonight, for some how I feel sad, and why it is I don't know. Everything is so different here, from the way I would like to have it. With the exception of the time I am with Mother, I am altogether alon—One has so much time to study that it has a tendency to make them despondent. I know you love me, for all I have done. I know you will trust me, and do everything you can to keep me from doing wrong; but the thoughts of having done wrong hurts me more than I can tell.

I don't intend to ever touch another drop of whisky; and to know you trust me has done more to keep me from it than anything else—No one else puts any confidence in me. When I said I would stop, they would as good as say they didn't believe it; and of course there was not much consolation in that.

I have turned over a new leaf;—but—there is still the old one glaring me in the face, with all its blots and crooked marks, which are so hard to erase from my mind, and forget. Pardon me—darling, if the tenor of this letter seems dull. I shouldn't have written when I feel blue; but I couldn't help writing to you, for you are my only thought—and I knew you would be looking for a letter from me. But there is a brighter day coming—when we shall be together; and no hand can separate us, save the one of whom bound us together; then our home will be a happy place.

When I look around at all the pictures it almost makes me think I am with you, they all look so natural. But there is a missing face,—that of dear Momma—Tell her to send me her picture soon; so I will have my family circle complete.

Write to me soon, darling, for I am so anxious to hear how you are. And if you should get any worse, let me know just as soon as possible; and I will come right away.

Give Momma and all the family my love. And with more than words can tell for you, my own darling.

I am your ever
                    Loving and devoted
                              Ham.

Please excuse this bad writing

M.V. Britannic
5 - 5 - 39.
Friday

My own Dearest Nikki.

I've just got to the breaking point
about your complete silence to me for these last 2 months
any I have different places to try and gather any
news regarding yourself, with complete failure and
many disapiontments to which I've completely in the
dark regarding your att atatude towards me darling
you just got to believe any never doubt that I do love
you and you alone and what ever you hear or
recieve about me please write me about it because
when a girl wants to get married to a guy and
then the guy heres no more something is wrong and
wants fixing up. If you feel that you dont still
love me and that there might be some one else, for
Gaol's sake please be open and write me, I'll under
stand allthough it will hurt like hell but
any thing is better than this worrying and no
news. Dad and I have had a hury serious now
and I am not to sure just what I intend doing in

in the near future, ~~this now and~~ I and I shall not be seeing
my Uncle again to often as of some differences we've had, and
what-ever your plans and an's are, will decied my plans
as I should & will look forward very much to hear as
I've never been soon fed up and lonly in all my life
and I intend to go to hell and the limit to try and
forget some of these hard heart-break's I've had
balle lately these last past few months and I'm not
standing for any more in the future, so please darling if
you still have a little feeling for me will you write
either to London or New York. we arrive in London on
the May 15 to 17 and June 9 to 11, and New York on the 25th
May for one day and then June 18th to 24 these are a few off
sailing dates, so please my darling let me hear something
and relieve my pain a little.

            I am and allways will be
        your truly loving husband for ever
                till the end
                        Nabby
                        x x x x x
                        x x x x
                            x x

I do hope you have
received my past-letters
a platograph I sent
to Mexics.

Dag:-

Just a few lines to let you know
how I feel. Oymar I can pardon a smouth
but I certainly can not pardon a lier, so If you
desire to hold me you had better come clean
and tell me the whole truth about everything

Maybe you can explain things last night, I
hope so, because you have nearly killed me.
Mag, I believed in you so much, I that you
were true, only to have it all dashed on the
rocks. Lord you will never know how I feel
to-day. And last night, god, my heart just
sank. When I first saw you, you I was
across the street. Hank was leaning against
the archway and you were standing up
close to him, oh so close, and he kept nodding
his head forward almost brushing your cheek.
You never pulled back at all. The girls were
not nere you two, either. Then when
I crossed the street and came down, you
had moved to where I caught you and
Hank was standing close to you with his
back to the other girls. You two were certainly
intimate and one could never tell by

Dag:

Just a few lines to let you know how I feel. Dagmar I can pardon a sneak but I certainly can not pardon a lier, so if you desire to hold me you had better come clean and tell me the whole truth about everything.

Maybe you can explain things last night, I hope so, because you have nearly killed me. Dag, I believed in you so much. I thought you were true, only to have it all dashed on the rocks. Lord you will never know how I feel to-day. And last night, god, my heart just sank. When I first saw you, I was across the street. Hank was leaning against the archway and you were standing up close to him, oh so close, and he kept nodding his head forward almost brushing your cheek. You never pulled back at all. The girls were not nere you two, either. Then when I crossed the street and came down, you had moved to where I caught you and Hank was standing close to you with his back to the other girls. You two were certainly intimate and one could never tell by looking at you that you could possibly have a steady. Lord, Dag can you explain that? However if you like Hank and have been false to me I would rather know as I can forgive that, much faster than if you lie to me. And Dag don't you realize that after trusting and believing in you the way I have only to find you are a sneak, that I can never have faith in you again, unless I am terribly mistaken about it all.

Please come clean Dag for it would certainly make me happy if you were mine after all. I don't see how I can believe that again tho.

Lord I hope you are satisfied now that you have broken my heart for I love you Dagmar.

Val

July 3rd

Victor, My Love —

My first thoughts as I awaken
in the morning, and the last as I
go to sleep at night. How greatly
blessed — to find you. You know certain
thoughts are prayers — I keep thinking —
'Thank You — every moment — for all of
the remaining years of my life.'
And Thank You, Victor, for opening the
door to the true heart of faith — I
am aware that I do not have the
right to ask for — or deserve to receive —
but can you find in your heart —
forgiveness for the long lonely years
of suffering which I caused for you?
I truly try to think what it must
have been — I don't have any answer
to why I made my decision as I did —
I only know — that I have never
stopped regretting hurting you — and
you have never, one moment, been
really away from my heart. I would
not have found you had this not been true.
Thank you for releasing for me —

Victor, My Love

My first thoughts as I awaken in the morning, and the last as I go to sleep at night. How greatly blessed—to find you. You know certain thoughts are prayers—I keep thinking—'Thank you—every moment—for all the remaining years of my life.' And Thank You, Victor, for opening the door to the true heart of Faith—I am aware that I do not have the right to ask for—or deserve to receive—but can you find in you heart—forgiveness for the long lonely years of suffering which I caused for you? I—truly—try to think what it must have been—I don't have any answer to why I made my decision as I did—I only know that I have never stopped regretting hurting you—and you have never, one moment, been really away from my heart—I would not have found you had this not been true.

Thank you for releasing for me—suppressed love which has never known fulfilment—for not making me feel that demonstration of sentiment is not necessary—a bit too pure—perhaps—or too dreamy, or old fashioned—and Thank you for not making me feel inadequate—although I should—My gratitude for security with you—because I know that you have always loved me. It has been a mutual, blessed, and tender love—which is most rare. Oh, Darling—I am so sorry—for all of the darkness—I want to be near you—to know that you are all right—and I want your arms around me—I am so comfortable there.

You know—Victor—I know persons who have been married for forty years who are really not right for each other at all—and know it—and are still married—That wouldn't be better—would it? We belong—together—and have for 38 years—although we have not really been married—We are one—We always have been—Let us always be.

Sunday A.M.

I couldn't sleep from 3 until around 6 o'clock. In those hours, I was aware of many positive thoughts. I am very grateful for my belief again—it was buried, you know. My Father would be most happy to know that I am living—again—the name which he gave me. He was a man of deep feelings and wisdom, and must have known that I would need something special—and I know what he expected of me. It is most wonderful—in the still of the night—in the many turns on my pillow—to say "Please God, take care of my Darling," and know that you will be watched over—as you have been for so many years.

I trust you completely, Victor—and believe in you so much, that I shall not ask any questions. It will all be your way—and therefore the right way. I do have one request—a bit later.

I know that you love me and although I have not heard the spoken word for sometime—I know that I am your Sweetheart, and shall always be.

I love you,
Faith

Guess who!

October 23rd.
about 2 P.M.

Most Beloved Wife,

Today was a delightful event for me as your past 5th registered letters came, some dating back to August. I was like a kid again and felt closer to you than I have in a long time, reading your very own handwriting and your wonderful thoughts as only you, my darling, can express them. I got your Aug 22nd Sept 6th, Aug 29th (with gremlin) and above all the others, your Sept 14th 11:45 Sex life letter. I eagerly read and reread all references to positive and intend rereading many more times. But more immediately important to us, aside from our little positive, is your Sept 14th letter. It was without comparison your most stimulating, revealing and most loved letter I can remember receiving since I left you. It opens so many problems that I knew existed but never discussed, and even as a love letter is unique, I'm sure unlike a love letter any husband ever received.

I wish I could say this to you by word of mouth, perhaps under a shady tree or

Most Beloved Wife,

Today was a delightful circus for me as your past 4 registered letters came, some dating back to August. I was like a kid again and felt closer to you than I have in a long time, reading your very own handwriting and your wonderful thoughts as only you, my darling, can express them. I got your Aug 22 and Sept 6TH, Aug 29TH (with gremlin) and above all the others, your Sept 14TH 11:45 sex life letter. I eagerly read and reread all references to positive and intend rereading many more times. But more immediately important to us aside from our little positive, is your Sept 14TH letter. It was without comparison your most stimulating, revealing and most loved letter I can remember receiving since I left you. It opens so many problems that I knew existed but never discussed, and even as a love letter is unique. I'm sure unlike a love letter any husband ever received.

I wish I could say this to you by word of mouth, perhaps under a shady tree or during our quiet warm moments next to each other after we are in bed and the lights are out, or just any place as long as we are together. But like all else we have to put our most intimate thoughts on paper and I know mine are inadequately expressed.

The episode at the "river bed" left me with much to regret because I realize now that if you had but suggested what is in your mind that you were thinking "below the belt" as you expressed it, it could have been one more of our never forgetable memories. I wish so you had dar-

ling, that you had followed your impulses. Please promise me that if that urge comes again at any place any time, you will tell me about it. You know my expression that when you get the old urge, by all means follow it. That was the girl I married and I loved you for it. But ever since you ceased to be "that girl" and became Mrs. Holmes, you became embarrased at the time I least expected you to. I was surprised but recognized it immediately and it followed through. I was trying in my clumsy subtle way to educate you away from it. I don't know whether you recognized it or not but there were times when I wanted to say "it is all very well and in the best custom for the male to be agressive, but not always the agressor. With all your liberalism, and our complete sharing, it is your right to demand me when you so desire. There is nothing in the book about it but then we never did follow the book did we! Complete co-ordination at all times is hard and I don't know whether we should reach it for quite some time, so if you have the urge, tell me and I shall be convinced oh so easily." That has been the way I felt but your very embarassment stopped me and I didn't know what to tell you. Now we know chief and it is so important that we do live that way. We are definitely not conventionalists and _never_ shall be regardless of how many children we have. There shall always be the original us a bit apart from our family yet without detracting from our family life. Those mutual moments, _regardless_ from whom the stimuli comes, are precious, and as we now see so regretably, incapable of being re-acted. Once we pass them by they are gone. How happy I was to know you felt that way! The "river bed" keeps going through my mind and I shall not cease regretting it. There is but one "out" as I remember (being the practical ass I am) you did not have your diaphram which at that stage would have been fatal. Let's make this our habit from now on. That we communicate all and every desire to each other (in the most lecherous manner possible?) irrespective of time or place and that you, darling, keep the old birth control gadget with you on all occasions. That's all expressed rather matter-of-factly and perhaps too baldly but in practice it will mean so much happiness and ultimate satisfaction to us both. We must admit that was one of our complete sharing plans that failed, or rather say we did not have time to develop it. It's a very essential part of our love, if not the basis and I should have talked it over with you much before this. Forgive me darling for it was my duty to acclimate my virgin wife in all ways and you were truly virginal at the darndest times. Nor can I boast of my patent qualities for I regret-ted the several moments that you flatly came out and told me I could do better. It was true but henceforth I am a wiser sage with experience behind me and my wife shall be a happier person for it. I admit she is also a little spoiled and it might be better if I kicked her teeth in occasionally but I rather think that becoming a mother will give her a sense of responsibility I'm sure she has. However, if she should become a conventional mother, and her second baby becomes all consum-ing interest, she will really have a fight on her hands for I do not expect her to change from the garrulous, impractical, impulsive, unconventional, girlish person I married, nor do I fear she will. Its consoling when I look into the future to know in my heart and mind that we shall be happier and as in the past, our love shall blossom even into a fuller bloom than it has, or than we suspect it will.

When our love is at stake you may rest assured your stinky will assert himself. I can han-dle it too for I know the subject matter; every crack (my my) and crevice of the body, mind, and actions of my most precious possession, you my darling and I don't propose losing what I shall never have again, or never be able to replace. I have "heard" you dearest, today if not on the 15TH of September and I too, as I have written before, cry out for you, not audibly, but with the telepathy of the mind that we must posses. Those gay, wild, moments shall come again be it on horseback or in the saddle. Your mention of your delightfully distorted pregnant body is all the more aggravating and when I talked the situation over with "Peter" he was very responsive but of necessity dormant. Could you ever believe again that you would shock me with your eagerness?

God has been good to me, to us, in the very unity of our lives. I am humble in his pres-ence as never before and my prayers are nevercessingly made in behalf of my muchly loved wife and our pending family. I think he looks at our personal life kindly and understandingly and sort leaves it up to us to dictate. Anything that can bring us as much happiness as we have given to each other in our elations must be alright with Him. We have confessed before God and the world that we are husband and wife and that each others welfare comes before all else. Surely he must bless our efforts at love making and I trust he hears my daily prayers on behalf of my most precious possessions and gives them the strength and guidance I ask. Just as surely he shall guide us back together again for he must know that is all we live for.

Hope this reaches you near your birthday remember your stinky husband loves you muchly and is thinking of you especially that day.

Happy Birthday my darling and
      To hell with propriety
            your carnal husband

Rout 2 Box 107
Saturday Night.

My Dearest Sweetheart Phil:
Oh my God, - this
sure is a dog's life. Believe
thow me kid I will stay
here Just long enough to
lay up a Couple of hundred
dollars, & then by hell I am
Gone. That is if I don't get
that jive Job. Of course if
I get that I will be O.K.
Your dear sweet letter
of last Sunday & Monday
reached me safely today.

My Dearest Sweetheart Phil:

Oh my God,—this sure is a dog's life. Believe thou me kid I will stay here just long enough to lay up a couple of hundred dollars, and then by hell I am Gone. That is if I dont get that fire job. Of course if I get that I will be O.K.

Your dear sweet letter of last Sunday and Monday reached me safely today. I sure was more than glad to get it too. I have read it over 3 times. You see honey,—I am—just exsisting and that is all. Sick enough to be in a hospital, but working anyway. I can't lay abed and awake, as I get to thinking and thinking and nearly go nuts, so I get up and go to work. Honey lover if it were not for you I would go crazy I believe. I dont go any where or see anything but work and more of it. Here I am getting up at 3 in the morning. Striping out 68 cows, eat breakfast and work in field till 11. Then come in and sleep for 1 hour. Eat dinner and rest a little and then it is 1 oclock. Then get the first two strings of cows in and wash them and feed them and then it is time to milk again. It is 5 or 5:30 when we get thru, then it is to eat supper and go to bed so as to get up again at 3 and do the same thing over again. Well I just got thru taking a darn good dump, so I feel that much better anyway. No I will tell you Honey,—I dont want to be for ever singing the Blues, but honestly I have not been satisfied since I left B.V. and you. Well I pray that things wont always be this way.

—Sunday—

Well I wonder how my Dearest one is today. A year ago today I knew how you were, and a year from today I pray that I can be saying to my friends "Meet my Wife." Ha ha kind of makes you smile a bit now dont it?

Oh there is one thing here and that is that there sure is a nice bunch of men here. They seem to like me and try to do every thing they can for me. They always come in my bunk at night and sit and talk for an hour or so. Of course I have your picture on the table here so that helps to draw them and I dont mean may be.

Dam the luck,—this morning when they called me at 3 I was dreaming that you and I were out walking and just going home as we saw the "lights go out." Ha ha. We just had got in the house and were sitting on the couch and going to —lay down, when—here they came and woke me. Say I would have given anything for another 5 minutes sleep. Haha. In other words I came near to have a "Wet Dream." Haha. Well such is life in the far west.

I sure would have liked to heard Leadbeater again. Say wont fellows talk when they see me back again? Haha.

No you darn right I have not got the right kind of "tits" to pull, but I wont try any "funny" stuff with Evelyn nor any other shemale until I get you, cause I sure know how I would feel to think of any other man or boy laying their

<u>hand on you</u>. It makes me sick to even think of it, I recon it has the same affect on you to think of me doing it with any one else, so I am 100% true to you.

Am sure relieved to know you are <u>not</u> going back with Lumbs. You sure are a prince of a Sweetheart not to get sore at me nor think I am crabby. Gosh Lover I sure do love you and can hardly wait till you are with me.

Well Lover I guess that I have about run down, so will shut up. Say how do you like your watch? Did Mr. or Mrs. Brann see it? if so what did they say.

Dont forget to tell me who is "K.M." and how Evelyn F. and Frank P. are coming.

Well honey it is about time to milk again, and then I am going to church at Van Nuys, so I will say good bye. With all my love and kisses.

Yours always,
Lee

QUEEN'S HOTEL,
SOUTHSEA.

8·45 P.M. Thursday. 21ˢᵗ Sept. 1944.

My Darling—
　　　　　The cab rolled away &
"man" receded into the distance, & then
you were gone . . . . . When I eventually
recovered my self control I realised
that the "cabbie" was eyeing me through
the small mirror — He winked & said-
"Husband going out to sea?" For a
few minutes I couldn't say a word,
so I just nodded . . . . . then, "he is
not my husband, but . . . ." "He said ——
"I know — I guess he soon will be"!
At which remark I grinned from ear-to
-ear & said he was quite right, &
dearest, you will probably have an
idea just what a thrill it gave me

My Darling—

The cab rolled away and "Man" receded into the distance, and then you were gone… When I eventually recovered my self control I realized that the "cabbie" was eyeing me through the small mirror—He winked and said "Husband going out to sea?" For a few minutes I couldn't say a word, so I just nodded… then, "he is not my husband, but… " "He" said—"I know—I guess he soon will be!" At which remark I grinned from ear-to-ear and said he was quite right, and dearest, you will probably have an idea just what a thrill it gave me to be able to say that! We made "small talk" for a "wee" while, and then he came out with another remark—"You've picked a good 'un, missie, I know a fine fellow when I meet one; leastways I should do, seeing as how I've been driving cabs around nigh on thirty five years now, and meeting people all them years I can soon size 'em up!!" Gosh, sweetheart, I could have hugged him for saying that—I felt so thrilled! He contin ued: "I'm not saying that 'cos you're going to marry him, I can just tell… me and my misses was married for thirty two years (God bless'er) and I lost her a month before the war—I've not been the same man since then; we never had a cross word, yes, missie, them was 'appy years, and I hope as how you tow young'uns have the same!" (End of what the cabbie said—we had arrived at the hotel entrance) I tootled around to the "dear soul" at the desk, and advised her I would be leaving on the 10:20 A.M. tomorrow, asked for a cab etc., then, being at the "end of my tether" (if you know what I mean, honey) I dashed up to my room and after releasing all the pent-up emotion due to our parting, darling, I tidied up (once again), and eventually commenced my lonely meal downstairs about eightish. At the moment I am having coffee in the lounge and trying to pen a few thoughts to my darling so he can know that I love him with all my heart, and I honestly do not know how I am going to exist without seeing him and being held tightly in his arms. Every day we're apart Fred, will seem like a lifetime to me, and I'm hoping that October will see "us" together again.

9:45 P.M. Continued.

My Darling, do you remember I had a date with you about this time? Well, here I am sitting in "R" chair. I have just read your letter and opened the "surprise parcel." And I am simply "full up to the brim" with love for you, gosh, how I wish you were here so I could thank you for this bracelet, sweetheart, it is a delightful present. Of course, I just had to fit it around my wrist to get "the effect." Really darling, when I think of everything you have done for me these past five days, it seems I shall never be able to thank you sufficiently—or to tell you how much I appreciate every thoughtful considerate action of yours—gee, I think you're "a man in a thousand," and I respect and love you for—"yourself"! Good-night, dearest, I'm going to have a bath and retire to my "lonely couch." I miss you terribly and can hardly wait until we are: Mr. & Mrs. F.W.S.

Muriel

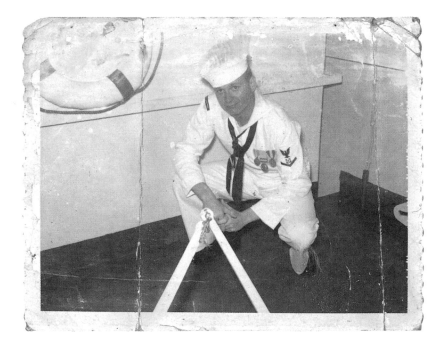

Mrs. Cowart do you think
you no how much I love
you.
  Well you don't and you
never Swell!

      Happy

        Anniversary

"Daddy"   Darling

Kenton McCoy

My Dear Maurine:-

A cloud has come over my young life and the
curtain of night drapes it enshrouding folds around my tender
limbs and I shudder lest the rising sun of to-morrow may not
kiss the dew from the lips of day or the noon-day meal be
partaken with my lady love.

For a report has come unto your beloved one
that men are marching upon the town to enquire of the character
and worldly standing of your Knight Errant and requests my
humble presence in the city of our dear beloved and much
admired and absent Maurine.

And even as if to add to the engulfing sorrow
which besets me now and augment the sad refrain, it is decreed
that you shall bear the burden of the great intelegence which
I am soon to impart, for it is none to soon to predict that
the big show will be fully housed under our own canvas even as
the day approaches and shall come to pass - none to soon.

Meaning in Stars And Stripes, that a wire
just received states that our Pittsburg people (two) who have
been in Tulsa for several days are returning home by way of
Denver and ask that I see them on Saturday, which I am glad
and not glad to do, all of,which will be more fully said when
I talk with you this evening and as for the large show business
I will more fully explain later, only I feel it coming over
me and the closer I get to it the less its frightfullness
appals me.

As a stimulus for a mental gymnast I commend
the noon-day lunch at the D. A.C. from which place I have
just return and for the first time since early spring, but
the omelette was good.

I am using Websters Collegiate which will
account for any errors that may occur in this letter, but I
hope to be able to fully explain when I see you, what I am
trying to say here, howbeit that if my friends keep me here
after the noon train Saturday I will come down on the S. Fe.
at 3.45 Saturday, but if it is possible to get away at noon
"thirty" I will come and find you when I get there.

This is a beautiful Kem day and I wish we
were all together, together - but I will be there almost as
soon as these lines and quite as alive.

Many kinds of affection of which I have never
written before --

Always yours,

Kenton

Denver, Colo.,
Saturday morning
Oct. 18, 1919.

My great big Goblin!

I found it —
and although I coaxed and
coaxed the saucy little brown
bow to tell me how and
when they got in my music
bench, and threatened not to
untie him from his box of
bondage and let loose his
harem of sweets in my parlor until he did tell me,

My great big Goblin!

I found it—and although I coaxed and coaxed the saucy little brown bow to tell me how and when they got in my music bench, and threatened not to untie him from his box of bondage and let loose his harem of sweets in my parlor until he did tell me, still he refused, and it was only my great insight of the goblin mind that enabled me to guess the goblin at the bottom of the pretty plot, but you are discovered, and your punishment shall await you at the station upon your return. Ah! Woe is you! You are the sweetest boy in the whole wide world, and I love you dearly.

Your darling Halloween card from Kansas City came this morning too before breakfast, and yesterday when I arrived home from the depot at one-thirty the telephone was ringing and I got your nice wire from Tulsa saying you were feeling fine and had had a nice trip.

I met Bert at 1:15 yesterday (Friday) and took a friend of his up to the Browns and we came home as I had dinner all prepared in case he should not have eaten, but as he had taken a bite at the Springs he did not care for anything, and so while I ate my lunch he told me about his good trip and drank a cup of tea.

After lunch we went down to the Savoy but he was unable to get a room as they had a full house and waiting list, and as he had stopped at the Adams before, he thought he would like a room there—which he was able to get—326 on the front. He went up and shaved while I waited in the car, and when he came down, as he had no business he wanted to attend to, we started for a drive.

We drove out to inspiration point and all over, and finally landed in Washington Park, and just when we had both come to the conclusion that the car was riding hard, another passed us and a man shouted "Your left hind wheel is flat" and flat she was, with a screw in her with a head the size of a dime—I think the largest souvenir we have ever picked up, and it is still in there it is stuck so tight.

Herbert got out and spent a half hour or more changing wheels, while I ate candy, and then after a little more driving we came home for supper. While I prepared it he played the Victrola, and after supper I played the Piano and we sang some, and about eight o'clock he suggested we go to a show, so we hopped in the car and went down to the Orpheum.

It was jammed and we had our choice between box and 12 row in the balcony, but after a conference in which we decided to try a box, the fellow very nicely sold Bert 2 seats, center, the parquet, which were fine, and the show was pretty good. We put the car up and Bert walked home with me and took a street car down town.

He said he would tend to his business this morning and phone me about noon, and he has asked me to have dinner down town with him tonight. This is a great deal about what I've been doing, isn't it, Honey Dear, but I know you'll swap stories and tell me all about your doings.

We both wondered how you were spending the time last night, and wished you were here with us.

Herbert was glad to hear of the Riverbed sale, and I surely hope things move swiftly and surely for you, and that there are no unforseen delays.

And now Honey Dear I'll fly around and get myself and my house presentable by noon, and write my Darling again tomorrow.

With worlds of love and deepest affection, bye-bye till tomorrow

Devotedly
Patsy

Jan 10. '4 [?]

Dear Miss Higbee

If I could link a mag-
netic wire from my brain
to yours, you would have a
very long electric letter, full
of gossip, news & nonsense,
with a little dash of tenderness — (this last item
inevitable) — but writing is
my daily load of which
the last ounce that breaks
my camel's back is a
private note. I love to
talk to you — I groan to
write to you. But you
know this as you know Every
thing else.

A thousand thanks
for your New Year's remembrance. There was in it

Dear Miss Higbee

If I could link a magnetic wire from my brain to yours, you would have a very long electric letter, full of gossip, news and nonsense, with a little dash of tenderness—(this last item is inevitable)—but writing is my daily load of which the last ounce that breaks my camel's back is a private note. I love to <u>talk</u> to you—I groan to <u>write</u> to you. But you now this as you know every thing else.

A thousand thanks for your New Year's remembrance. This made it a valuable compliment from a woman like you, and I and my paper take from it joy and courage. I may own to you, that I throw aside my better capabilities with so valiant an effort to scribble for that paper, that I value applause for it ten times more than I do for better things. If I have succeeded in pleasing such as you with it, I have "taken up my cross" to some purpose.

Well—God help you during 1849! I trust we shall be here to exchange kind messages I love the Doctor, for many another year. Here or elsewhere, however, believe me, dear Miss Higbee

Yours Most Sincerely,
N. P. Willis